Part of My Soul Went with Him

WINNIE MANDELA

Part of My Soul Went with Him

Edited by Anne Benjamin

and Adapted by Mary Benson

W · W · NORTON & COMPANY · NEW YORK LONDON

First American Edition, 1985

Portions of the book have appeared in *Mother Jones* and *Ms.* magazines.

ISBN 0-393-02215-3

ISBN 0-393-30290-3 pbk.

W. W. Norton & Company, Inc., 500 Fifth Avenue, New York, N.Y. 10110
W. W. Norton & Company, Ltd., 37 Great Russell Street, London WC1B 3NU

6   7   8   9   0

CONTENTS

EDITORIAL NOTE

This is not an autobiography in the conventional sense. The restrictions placed on her activities by the government and her daily involvement in the liberation movement make it impossible for Winnie Mandela to sit down and write a book. In any case, she dislikes talking about herself: it is not she who is important, she would say, but the struggle.

Winnie Mandela granted me the privilege of conducting lengthy tape-recorded interviews with her over a considerable period of time. She also entrusted me with letters from her husband in jail and other documents for selection, editing and publication. This book was compiled outside South Africa, and although Mrs Mandela was fully informed about the project, she could not see the manuscript in detail before it went into print. The same applies to the other people interviewed for the book. Thus the responsibility for the editing of interviews, for the selection of documents and for any mistakes and omissions is mine.

I wish to express my great gratitude and appreciation to Mary Benson, a long-time friend of the Mandela family and author of a biography of Nelson Mandela, for her invaluable improvements and editorial advice, especially regarding the history of the ANC and the life of Nelson Mandela.

Anne Benjamin
September 1985

PHOTOGRAPHIC ACKNOWLEDGEMENTS

Thanks are due to the following for the photographs: Peter Magubane (1, 2, 3, 7, 8, 11, 12, 13); Mary Benson (10); Amina Frense (5). Photographs 4 and 6 are by Anne Benjamin.

INTRODUCTION

You take the plane from Johannesburg to Bloemfontein, the capital of the Orange Free State, when you want to pay a visit to Winnie Mandela. For the last forty miles from the airport to Brandfort you hire a car. I nearly always go by plane; it is too far to drive if you want to be back in Johannesburg on the same day. Brandfort is about three hundred miles away and the roads are none too good.

The road from Bloemfontein to Brandfort crosses a stretch of countryside with a charm all its own; an open plain, stretching as far as the eye can see, occasionally broken by a few flat-topped mountains. It is one of the earth's geographical whims – these curious high plateaux scattered over the vast plain of the Orange Free State. Now and then you see one of the huge clusters of trees which protect the farms from the scorching summer sun as well as from the icy winter storms. There are huge stretches of grassland, with here and there lonely water-pumps whose wheels move in the wind and impose their monotonous rhythm on the whole countryside. In the evening they are silhouetted against the red sunset, bringing to life the unique poetry of this empty landscape. It is the typical *platteland*, the very centre of the Afrikaner territory, the Orange Free State.

I have travelled this road to Brandfort many times, at different times of the day and at different seasons, but this part of the country always remains the same – somewhat too austere, with its hard, shadowless contours, almost as if there were no life in it, no change, no time. Perhaps this is what one of my friends meant when he called this countryside 'archaic' and added: 'It fits the people.'

Indeed, when the Orange Free State was founded in 1854 as an independent Boer republic, one group of settlers actually wanted the original law of Moses to be made part of the new constitution.

The farmers, who live widely separated along the road to Brandfort, who, like their forefathers, breed cattle and sheep, and whose family names are Pretorius or Uyl or Retief or Potgieter – they are convinced that this part of Africa was uninhabited before they took possession of it, that 'Almighty God ... who has guided them from generation to generation; who has wondrously delivered them from the dangers that beset them', gathered their 'forebears together from many lands and gave them this for their own'. This is what the preamble to the South African Constitution says, and the Boers believe every word of it. No historian, not even reality itself, can teach them otherwise.

They should have known that the land was not 'uninhabited' back in 1836. Dr Andrew Smith, the leader of an official expedition sent out by the British administration of the Cape Colony, had made a detailed report of conditions in the tableland of what is now the Free State: the area was settled by various small ethnic groups, in a state of rising political tension; it was ruled by Ma Nthatisi, the widow of an influential Sotho chief, a 'woman of great intelligence, beauty and political talent'.

Brandfort is a typical small Afrikaner town; it is regarded as a 'white' town although the whites make up only a quarter of the total population: there are about 3,000 whites and 9,000 blacks. But the blacks, who are the original inhabitants and real owners of the land, have no role – their ghetto has no name, it is out of sight – just as Ma Nthatisi and her subjects played no part in the plans and calculations of the trekking Boers back in 1836.

If one tries to find out what it is that makes the Afrikaners cling so determinedly and desperately to the fiction that South Africa is a 'white' country, several reasons crop up again and again; the religious motive is at the forefront, yet closely connected with this are very profane motives indeed: greed, fear and the desire for power.

When the British prohibited the keeping of slaves and even started to think about a constitution which would give equal rights to all races, the Boers left the Cape. The niece of the leader of the trek, Piet Retief, expressed their views: 'And yet it is not so much their freedom which drove us to such lengths, as their being placed on an equal footing with Christians, contrary to the laws of God and the natural distinction of race and colour. So that it was intolerable for any decent Christian to bow down beneath such a yoke, wherefore we rather withdrew in order thus to preserve our doctrines in purity.' The situation today echoes these feelings: there are ten churches in the district of Brandfort, nine of them for whites only.

I came to Brandfort for the first time in 1977. I wanted to see the place which had been confronted with Winnie Mandela completely out of the blue, one day in May earlier that year. Had her arrival been, figuratively speaking, the long-overdue encounter between Piet Retief and Ma Nthatisi?

I drove past the town sign, past the Volksskool and the Andries Pretorius Park. I did not want to attract attention, so I parked the car intending to go to the centre on foot. It turned out, however, that I was already there: the very first road, which I thought I had turned into quite by chance, was in fact the main road – or rather the only road – in Brandfort, the Voortrekker Road.

On every visit to Brandfort I tried to fight off the anxiety I felt as soon as I passed the first few houses on this road; I tried to convince myself that the police cars continually driving up and down the Voortrekker Road were just part of the picture, as in any other South African town. If I, as a visitor for a few hours, felt defenceless and somehow exposed in this forsaken spot, what must be the feelings of the woman who has been living here for seven years now and who is under twenty-four-hour police surveillance?

There is not much to see in the town itself: a few shops on either side of the road, the Standard Bank and Barclays Bank, a police station, two small hotels, a post office, a petrol station, two churches, the beer-hall for the blacks, never missing in such places, and the pavement roofed over in simple colonial fashion. There are a few minor roads with bungalow-style houses, where the whites live. One supermarket, a newsagent's, the railway station a little farther on, and two huge grain silos at the end of the town – that's all.

Social life in Brandfort is not particularly varied. People meet each Sunday in church and make arrangements for a game of golf or a barbecue in the garden, the traditional *braaivleis* – there is no shortage of steaks. Once a year everyone takes part in the one and only important social event: the games in the school hall.

There is little danger of new, let alone liberal, ideas spreading in this sort of climate. In the whole of Brandfort only three copies of the liberal English *Rand Daily Mail*, now defunct, were sold each day; the supermarket, opened a few years ago, has managed to survive; a drive-in cinema which tried its luck in the area had to be closed due to lack of custom.

A sleepy, rural retreat if ever there was one. Until 1977, when Winnie Mandela arrived.

To this Afrikaner community, full of memories of a golden past – post offices with separate entrances for blacks and whites, pavements which immediately emptied of blacks when a white person came into sight – the government had banished the woman who symbolizes the black struggle for liberation. Doubtless they hoped that here her spirit of resistance would be broken and that – far removed from the centres of political tension in South Africa – she would gradually be forgotten.

Or could the opposite happen? Was it possible that this remote town way out in the Orange Free State might be roused from its idyllic peace and quiet by the mere presence of this extraordinary woman? 'That woman', the people in Brandfort say when they talk about Winnie Mandela, and it sounds like a propitiation – as if the evil spirit could be kept at bay as long as they do not call it by its proper name.

'I invaded the kingdom of the Afrikaners like a whirlwind,' Winnie Mandela laughs, 'and now they live in fear here in Brandfort.'

I met Winnie Mandela for the first time on the Voortrekker Road, in a tiny room in the office of her lawyer at that time, Piet de Waal. 'Go to De Waal and ask him to send a message to Winnie Mandela in the township telling her that you are waiting to see her in Brandfort' – this was what friends had advised me to do.

Whites are still not allowed to enter the township without a permit from the magistrate, and if the reason given for applying for such a permit is to visit Winnie Mandela, the answer is usually no.

I noticed a slight tension, a slight embarrassment when I turned up unexpectedly in the lawyer's office, but my request was complied with immediately.

How well I remember the bare, narrow room in which I waited, and my growing nervousness when the messenger sent to Winnie Mandela had not returned two hours later. Would she come in time, would she come at all, would we be able to talk in peace in this busy office atmosphere?

After all, I had not come for a simple interview – I was not looking for a few basic facts and figures. I wanted to ask Winnie Mandela – the woman, the mother, the political fighter – what gave her the strength to bear what she had borne: living under a ban for the greater part of her adult life, with countless arrests; imprisonment shortly after her marriage, while expecting her first child; constant surveillance for the last twenty-two years; cross-examination and torture; a marriage which during the last twenty years has consisted of nothing but censored letters, casual glances and brief conversations through the glass partition in the visitors' rooms of prisons under the watchful eyes of prison officers; separation from her husband and often from her children, family and friends as well.

She eventually arrived and stood in the doorway, very upright, full of spirit and infectious vitality; she had none of the outward signs of authority, but I sensed a very compelling personality. She wore a long, black and green African dress, and had a scarf draped around her head according to the Xhosa tradition; her clear and remarkably expressive face was a perfect mirror of the quick succession of her feelings. Her features were aristocratic: high cheek-bones and very big, dark, inquisitive eyes, which seemed to express a most fascinating mix of contradictory feelings: quiet sorrow, pain and, at the same time, unrestrained cheerfulness, ironic detachment and impish humour. It was this tension between the contradictions within her which fascinated me immediately: this closeness of laughter and sorrow, the obvious love of beauty, even though she had been through all the prison routine of interrogation and torture and had long given up all claims to a life of personal happiness.

With her open, welcoming smile she brushed aside all traces of strangeness and embarrassment between us, accepted the greetings and small presents I had brought from her friends with spontaneous joy and pleasure, and inquired enthusiastically about particular friends and acquaintances, always insisting on a detailed answer, for this was one of the few ways she could keep in touch with them.

I will never forget this conversation. A strange intensity made us skip all the intermediary phases of getting to know each other, and we touched on some of the vital issues of her life and her experience. Were there not times when she lost all hope and courage? When she felt nothing but resignation and despair? Her first answer came quickly, with an angry glance: 'Of course not. How can I lose hope when I know that in truth this country is ours and that we'll get it back! I know that all this is something I must bear in order to reach that goal.'

But then she fell silent, and her silence told of the forces against which she must fight continually. And in a husky tone – her voice is usually clear and melodious – she added: 'I am too small in this enormous liberation machine. Blacks are dying every day in this cause. Who am I to contribute my little life? The case before us is too great for me to even be thinking of what happens to me personally.' In these moments of silence I learnt perhaps more than from what she actually said; I got a glimpse of what lay behind her ready laugh, her warm and open manner. I felt very near to her and decided to return and get to know her better.

On my way back her words echoed in my mind and I tried to imagine what her life was like, a life regulated by a decree from the Ministry of Justice, beginning with these words: 'Whereas I, James Thomas Kruger, Minister of Justice, am satisfied that you engage in activities which endanger or are calculated to endanger the maintenance of public order, I hereby, in terms of section 9 (1) of the Internal Security Act, 1950, prohibit you . . .'* There follows a long list of all the regulations and restrictions which make up her life: she is not allowed to attend a school or a university, to visit a factory or even a nursery, to enter premises where any kind of publication is being prepared or produced or where a public gathering might be in progress; she is not allowed to address public meetings, to be with more than one person at a time. It is illegal for anyone in South Africa to quote anything she says. She told me with a laugh that she left the papers on the desk of the police officer when she was sent to Brandfort, but even if she herself tries to ignore the restrictions, the Security Police in Brandfort watch over

---

* See Appendix for full text.

her and see to it that the rules and regulations are adhered to to the letter.

I went to see Winnie Mandela many times after our first meeting. I always drove through 'white' Brandfort without stopping. A few hundred yards outside, the surfaced road stops and becomes a dusty, bumpy track winding slightly uphill to the 'boundary' between Brandfort and the black ghetto, which has no official name; 'Phathakahle' it is called by the inhabitants – 'to be handled with care'. I had several meetings with Winnie Mandela at this boundary line; it is not marked by any fence, but whites are not allowed to cross it without a permit – just an imaginary line across the road leading into the township. From it you can see the whole ghetto: almost a thousand houses, little greyish-yellow boxes, one exactly like the other, in monotonous rows; dusty mud roads with no lighting, no tarmac, no names; one shop, one school, one beer-hall, and that's it.

After torrential rainstorms the roads become almost impassable; every evening the township disappears under a screen of smoke from open fires and sooty paraffin lamps. It is a typical black location for workers, uniform and anonymous like white Brandfort itself. The building which houses the Bantu Administration dominates the scene; it is close to the imaginary line at the entrance to the township. Life in the ghetto is controlled from here and no one, whether visitor or inhabitant, passes through unnoticed.

I quite often waited for Winnie Mandela here. She was often late; sometimes she came in an old VW, sometimes on foot, sometimes alone, often in the company of two young men – friends of the family from Soweto – with a few youngsters from the township keeping a respectful distance: 'my bodyguards', she would say. The words also contained an ironic hint what her status would be in a 'normal' South Africa, a South Africa without apartheid, with Nelson Mandela in his rightful position as the blacks' chosen leader. And indeed, when she stood there on the dusty township road, very straight and very beautiful, wearing either a traditional Xhosa robe or European dress with an air of natural elegance, when she calmly ignored the Bantu Administration officers and came to sit in my car with three people at a time under their very eyes (even though this is prohibited in terms of her banning order), she was more like a brilliant ambassadress representing her country than the banned inmate of a ghetto in the back of beyond.

Her appearance reminded me of the words of a white friend of hers, who had once accompanied her on her way to prison: 'Winnie approached the prison like the Queen of Africa.'

It seemed as if she did not even notice the almost absurd contrast which her mere physical appearance created in this surrounding, as if she felt perfectly at home where she was, as if this township in Brandfort was the place for her to be, and as if her house, No. 802, was an appropriate place for her to welcome her prominent visitors from all over the world.

Whenever I saw her I looked in vain for any signs of despair or resignation. She had the unyielding attitude of the political fighter who puts up with even the most desperate circumstances without losing sight of her aim, who is not deterred by defeats and setbacks, but rather gains new strength from them.

Even her husband was surprised by the undaunted stamina with which Winnie Mandela settled down in Brandfort. She has become so engrossed in the projects she has started there that, in a letter to Nelson Mandela, she described the place of her banishment, with a touch of serene irony, as 'quite nice really', as if the hardships she has to cope with did not exist: spending hours every day cleaning her minute rooms of the dust which finds its way through the smallest nook and chink; being cut off from communication with all her friends; spending three hours every day in the post office in Brandfort, so that people can get in touch with her by telephone. There are times when her always precarious financial situation becomes desperate and she cannot even afford to buy paraffin for days on end. Above all there is the continual threat she lives under, the never-ending persecution by the Security Police and – not least – the moments of pain, want and loneliness.

And yet the sorrow I had seen in her eyes when we first met is an integral part of her. She is – and I loved her for this – not a 'heroic' woman: she has not become a single-minded political fighter, tough and immune, but has remained vulnerable.

In 1983 I got permission to see Winnie Mandela in her little house for the first time. I was informed by the authorities that the regulations were entirely for my own safety, and that if anything happened to me they would accept no responsibility. And so, at last, I came to her 'house' – she would not forgive me if I did not put the word in quotes;

she herself calls those three minute rooms – bedroom, kitchen, living-room, about thirty square metres in all – her 'prison cells'. She has managed, however, to make these 'cells' habitable. The tiny living-room is dark, but not uncomfortable, even though somewhat haphazardly furnished; most of her furniture was taken back to Soweto immediately after she arrived. The arms of the sofa are covered with rather touching little pieces of needlework, embroidered village scenes with hens and children, given to her by women from the neighbourhood.

On a shelf there is a small battery-operated TV; there is also a great variety of books given to her by various people, roughly catalogued on pieces of cardboard. Those in the ghetto interested in reading can borrow from her Joseph Conrad, Saul Bellow's *Rain King*, volumes on British history, or the *Prophet* by Gibran.

The rows of medicine bottles which used to be there have now disappeared. A neat little prefabricated house, financed by money from various donations, has been erected in her garden as a 'clinic' for the inhabitants of the ghetto, and she no longer has to treat patients in her house or garage.

When you leave the house you find yourself in a garden filled with flowers. What used to be rubble and dust is now covered in flowerbeds and bushes. In the shade of a willow tree, which offers protection against the sun and the watchful eyes of the policemen living next door, I was reminded of the words of Sally Motlana, who once described Winnie Mandela's strength: 'They will never succeed in building a wall around her. It doesn't matter where they banish her – homeland, desert or forest – this woman is so dynamic, she will make the birds sing and the trees rustle wherever she goes. You can be sure of that.'

A TRIBUTE TO NOMZAMO WINNIE MANDELA

by Bishop Manas Buthelezi, President of the South African Council of Churches, Bishop in the Lutheran Church of South Africa

'Nomzamo Mandela is more than just another black person. In a very mystic way, she sums up in her life experience almost all that laws like the Suppression of Communism Act and Terrorism Act have in store for those who have voiced their abhorrence of the policy of apartheid. It is common knowledge that she has been subjected to systematic harassment, banning, detention and imprisonment, an ordeal which even very few charged and convicted common-law criminals have been made to endure.

'In a very deep sense she qualifies for the title of being "The Mother of Black People". I am not saying this simply because she happens to be the wife of her husband who is one of the imprisoned leaders of black people, but also because of what she has become in her own right.

'I belong to a religion which teaches that salvation or liberation is via the cross of suffering and that through the suffering of one the liberation of many was secured. I am sure that even in other religions there are elements of this teaching.

As far as human experience is able to go Mrs Mandela has tasted what redemptive suffering means. She has suffered and has been punished not because of corrupt and criminal traits in her character and conduct but because her life personifies the black man's struggle for justice and liberation. She has suffered because you and I deserve more than the South African way of life is able to give us. Her suffering is the measure of our worth as human beings and of her love for us. In the Christian Bible it reads: 'There is no greater love than this, that a man should lay down his life for his friends' (John, XV, 13).

'If anyone is in doubt of Nomzamo Mandela's love for her people and for South Africa as a whole let him look at what she has endured.

'Perhaps someone may be surprised why I lay so much emphasis on the aspect of suffering in Mrs Mandela's life. I do so because there are many people who do a lot of talking without counting the cost they may be called upon to pay as a consequence. Very often when such people are confronted with the reality of the stand they have taken they quaver and quiver to the point of marching right about turn. Mrs Mandela stuck to her guns to the end.

'I do so also for another reason. You never get something for nothing. A cause that fails to produce leaders of the stuff martyrs are made of cannot hope to achieve its aims. It is only great religions which have produced leaders of such high moral integrity that they were able to endure the test of the fire of persecution at the hands of their enemies and detractors.

'Mrs Nomzamo Mandela should be counted among such great heroes. I would be failing in my duty if I neglect to mention that besides Mrs Mandela there are many others who are suffering. There are many who are still banned, detained and imprisoned as part of a political strategy to silence all opponents of apartheid who operate on platforms other than those provided by the institutions of separate-development politics. They are the lambs that have to be slaughtered in order to install the many mini-governments that are in the offing.

'Many of these are unknown to most of us. Perhaps no report of their story ever appeared in any newspaper. The tears of their relatives and the ruin that has been caused to their families as a result of this political circumstance have never been brought to the attention of the public. They are simply part of the nameless mass of banned and detained people. It is in this respect that personalities like Nomzamo Mandela come as a God-sent gift.

'I am persuaded by the above facts to say that I am happy that Mrs Mandela was banned too, detained too, and imprisoned too. Her name and stature have forced even some of the most apathetic to realize what is behind the reality of bannings, detentions and political imprisonments. Her imposing stature has served to make visible the statureless nobodies who are victims of these political evils somewhere in an unknown police cell or remote *bundu*, people who have a story to tell but with nobody who cares to carry it. Through the story of her own life we are able to read the story of many others. Her experience serves as a magnifying glass through which we are able to see important details of the experiences of others. She is a window through which even the most uninitiated eye is introduced to the obscure, twilight existence of the banned and detained. Through her the invisible were made visible. She was the type of a personality whom the press and other publicity media could not afford to forget even in her many years of statutory silence and non-existence. That is why I say that she was a gift of God for us all. She was and is the incarnation of the black people's spirit.

'Many of our leaders are now silent. Some are silent because they are dead and others because they are banned, detained or imprisoned. One thing the dead have in common with the banned and detained is that all of them are silent. They can no longer speak in order to be heard. Yet they can continue to communicate with us even through the medium of their silence. That is why nobody can stop the silenced ones from giving spiritual strength to the rest of us. Mrs Mandela has been silenced during all these many years. Yet her life has communicated more than all the speeches she could ever make if she had never been banned. I for one never heard her speak before she was banned, I had never even read anything she had said and written until for a brief time she was unbanned. Yet by intuition I could feel and hear her presence.

'While I was banned I had many possibilities of leaving the country and settling elsewhere. I did not do so because of people like Mrs Mandela who had been able to maintain their dignity and integrity under the circumstances of humiliation. My banning order was nothing compared to Mrs Mandela's. But she was able to build inner resources and spiritual strength so that even the harsh banning order was not able to break her and brain-wash her. She was silenced all right, but I heard her strengthening message and I was able to survive the banning order. I am sure that there are many banned people who have been strengthened by the example of Mrs Mandela.'

My Little Siberia

BANISHED TO BRANDFORT

'When they send me into exile, it's not me as an individual they are sending. They think that with me they can also ban the political ideas ... I couldn't think of a greater honour.'

It was the night of 16 May 1977. I was doing an assignment in sociology and, because I was working, I used to do my assignments at night – it took me right up to 2 a.m. There was a deadline. I had to submit something the following day. So I finished it at about half past two.*

I had been hearing strange noises outside. But then it's such a usual part of my life, that kind of thing. I've always known that I'm never alone wherever I am, so hearing footsteps outside was nothing new; I've lived like that with these people, I just thought the police were making their usual rounds outside. I switched off the lights but I couldn't fall asleep.

At about four o'clock in the morning I heard a great noise outside – it seemed as if a hail of stones were dropped on my house and it sounded

---

*I had a lot of academic wrangling with regard to my studies. They didn't let me complete my degree in social work here in the Free State. This is the first time a black woman had done sociology in the Free State. They said I must do a degree in arts, which I'm not interested in. I'm at present specializing in industrial and political sociology. I can't do that as a major when I do arts.

as if they were falling inside the wall – I've got this high cement wall around the house in Orlando.

In a fraction of a second there were knocks all over, on the doors, on all the windows, bang, bang, bang, bang-sounds. You would think they would ring the bell – no – simultaneous knocking on the door, barking, then I knew what was happening. I just took it for granted that I was under arrest. I thought as usual they were taking me under Section 6.*

I went and opened the door and of course I saw the whole army inside the yard, chaps in camouflage carrying guns, and members of the Security Branch; they were all heavily armed.

I always keep a suitcase packed with clothes because of the problems I've had in the past. I've always been detained alone – my children were usually in boarding schools. I have a suitcase ready, so that when I'm taken to prison nobody is going to have to struggle to find me – I have a set of clothes, toiletry, toothbrushes, combs.

I picked up that case. And then they said, 'You are under arrest.' There was the usual angry exchange. My daughter Zindzi was with me, and I wasn't prepared to leave her without exactly knowing how long I would be away. I never even had time to finish – I was whisked away, then I was taken to Protea police station.

There they tried to interrogate me, but if you have been inside as long as I have, you cannot go through that worthless exercise again. No policeman can come to me today at my age and think that he can still interrogate me. In my younger days it was different, but any squeak of a little policeman who came to question me today would just be wasting his time. We would just end up insulting each other, that's all. This went on for the rest of the morning till about ten o'clock. At ten o'clock I saw Zindzi escorted into the cell I was kept in with these heavily armed chaps, and she was carrying the house keys. And for the first time I realized what was happening. These three men who were in the same cell interrogating me simply stood up and said, 'You are now going to be banished to the Free State.' I hadn't the slightest idea of what was going on, I thought I was under arrest. From there I thought I was going to be moved either to Pretoria or to another of the country's

---

*The section of the Terrorism Act under which Winnie Mandela was held in 1969. It provided for indefinite, incommunicado detention while under interrogation.

prisons as usual. And when Zindzi came with these men it was the first time I realized I was being banished.

We were taken into one of these army trucks. Our every possession was there: they had ripped off bedspreads and sheets from the bed, they took everything, emptied the wardrobes and cupboards into those sheets, my crockery was tied up with the blankets, three quarters of course was broken into pieces, Nelson's books were bundled into bedspreads. Of course half the stuff got damaged.

Then we drove to the Free State, just like that. Zindzi and I were at the back between heavily armed men and there were others in front. And then of course there were other trucks escorting us. I had never even known that there was a place like Brandfort. We were dropped at the police station and handed over to the Security Branch of the Free State. They were all there in full force too.

From there we were driven to the house – in fact it's an insult to call these three cells a house – when we got there, there wasn't even room to enter – the soil took up three quarters of each little cell. They had to get men with shovels to scoop the soil from the rooms, they were so full of rubbish. What we subsequently gathered from the neighbourhood was that when they were building the so-called new houses for the area, the builders used that house for dumping all their rubbish. They threw some of our bundles on the floor; they couldn't get one single item of our furniture through the doors. Apparently the little doors that are used for these houses are what you normally use for toilets – that is why our furniture got stored at the police station.

That first night naturally we hadn't washed, there isn't a drop of water – suddenly our house in Soweto seemed like a palace; we didn't have a bucket, not even a morsel of food. We couldn't cook. There was no stove. We were just dumped between these four walls. It was bitterly cold. We cuddled up on one mattress to get some sleep.

It was terrible. For Zindzi it was a traumatic experience. Any man could have been broken by that type of thing. It was calculated to do just that. Worse things have happened to people in the struggle, but for a sixteen-year-old girl it was very hard to take. It was the hardest thing for me to take as a mother, that your commitment affects those who are very dear to you. That shattering experience inflicted a wound that will never heal. Of course I was bitter, more than I've ever been.

At first the people in the location were petrified. The so-called

Members of Parliament around here and the police had held meetings, and the people had been told that a big communist was coming and they were warned of the dangers of associating with such a person. They were told this is a woman who is going to tell you that you must fight for your land, she is going to tell you all the wrong things. And if ever you set a foot in her house, we will promptly arrest you and you will spend the rest of your life like her husband, whom we arrested and who is in prison for life. And they were told to restrain their children and when they send their children to the shops they must see to it that they don't come anywhere near the house.

But today the black thinking is: if a white man says something is bad, then it must be very good. Although they were frightened by that type of thing, it was the exact opposite. This has been the pattern with all these racial laws anyway. Once a black is told by a white man that something is bad, then it must be good and vice versa. That's what happened. We didn't have any bridges to build. As time went on, people came to know who we were and what the whole thing was all about – we never addressed the people. Little children started spontaneously giving the Black Power sign, that is how they greeted us when the police were gone. They would wake us up early in the morning and bring us little parcels of food – some beans or cabbage – of course during the day nobody would speak to us. But at night they came and expressed their solidarity. That's what happened.

And every one of them knew of Nelson. Every one of them.

I have ceased a long time ago to exist as an individual. The ideals, the political goals that I stand for, those are the ideals and goals of the people in this country. They cannot just forget their own ideals. My private self doesn't exist. Whatever they do to me, they do to the people in this country. I am and will always be only a political barometer. From every situation I have found myself in, you can read the political heat in the country at a particular time. When they send me into exile, it's not as an individual they are sending. They think that with me they can also ban the political ideas. But that is a historical impossibility. They will never succeed in doing that. I am of no importance to them as an individual. What I stand for is what they want to banish. I couldn't think of a greater honour.

BRANDFORT – WHITE*

I am a living symbol of whatever is happening in the country. I am a living symbol of the white man's fear. I never realized how deeply embedded this fear is until I came to Brandfort. Our struggle is no longer something that is far away. Here it is reality. Here they see this type of black who gets this type of visitor *they* never had. People from the international community, from all over the world, who take an interest in the life of this 'Kaffir'. And the government doesn't learn any lessons – I never saw as many foreign governments in my twenty years in Johannesburg as I have seen in exile in Brandfort.

The Afrikaner in the Free State – for him a black is something that sits on their tractor or plods behind their plough. What is more important to that farmer is his tractor and not that labourer; and if lightning strikes that man dead on that tractor, the first thing he'll run and check is the tractor. The corpse he'll look at afterwards. The movement was – physically – symbolized by my presence in the kingdom of the Afrikaner, throwing me here amongst them. I went into the shops no black went into, at the police station I used the white entrance, I went into the white side of the post office – there was nothing they could do. Sometimes the police station was full of farmers. When I went in there, they automatically made way, not because they were being respectful, but because I had to go in, in order to get out! And the black people watching this from outside thought it was absolute respect.

When I went to the supermarket there were these huge Afrikaans-speaking women. When they saw me they used to run out and stay out until I finished my shopping. The 'Bantus' didn't get into the supermarket, they had these little windows through which they were supposed to buy. But once I started shopping there, the blacks went in too, and then I would deliberately take an hour to get whatever I needed – even if it was only a piece of soap – and I enjoyed seeing these women waiting outside.

The whites are bound to ask questions and to discuss them at home.

---

*The white population in 1977 was 1,900. Brandfort was previously best known as the town which shaped the Afrikaner Nationalist identity of Dr Hendrik Verwoerd, architect of apartheid.

That's the only way I can conscientize* them. That's the only way they will know of the struggle. Nobody has conscientized the people here the way Jimmy Kruger has by sending me here. I could never have done that. Many white people here had never heard of the African National Congress. They had never heard of Nelson Mandela. Here now is a living symbol of what they have been kept away from, of what they kept being warned against.

What is a communist to these whites? A communist to them is somebody like me. And if communists are people who walk into white shops, who use the entrances for whites – then, of course, they don't want to have anything to do with that.

If they saw me walking in the street they used to give way. After the blacks started going to the supermarket to shop, even when I was not there, the whites made representations to the government to have me removed. They even invited Coetsee, the Minister of Justice, and held big meetings in the town hall. I read about it in the *Johannesburg Post*. I think they promised they would look into the matter but nothing came of it.

I was in hospital at the time and when I came back I jocularly said to my lawyer, 'I hear they don't want me here any more. Well, then you had better tell the Minister of Justice, if he wants to renew my banning order, it had better be Brandfort, because I'm not going anywhere else.'

I find my work here very fulfilling. They have reached a stage now where they realize they no longer have any place for me in the country – they honestly don't know what to do with me.

Slowly, the whites here are becoming more aware of the deeper social issues. They never bothered about the living conditions of the 'Bantu' over the mountain there. Now the people have the confidence they never had before; the farmers used to stand with their lorries in town – they didn't even go into the township to find people to work on their farms – and the lorries would be full in five minutes with twenty or thirty 'Bantu' because people are unemployed. That has come to an end. The farmers have to go to the labour office now. The blacks know what their value is, they know their worth, even though there are no jobs. They have been so conscientized, they are no longer prepared to

*Politicize.

go and work for starvation wages. They used to work for 50c a day – you will not find a single one today who will work for that since we came here.

The highest wage in Brandfort was R10 a week – and that's the élite; the shops pay R5 or R8 a week. The people would rather stay in the township than work for that.

There have been quite a few changes in Brandfort. The blacks no longer stand in front of these silly little windows, and some shops had to close them.

All I have done is behave differently. And today, when people see that I do something, they also do it. Only the post office is still segregated and only workers from the farms way out in the rural areas still use the black entrance. All others use the main entrance. Even little things like that sometimes have significance. Imagine thirty people waiting while one white is being served.

I remember an instance in Foschini, the only fashion shop in Brandfort, and it is not even owned by Afrikaners. Just imagine how blacks were being served there: they must stand in the door and point out to the madam: can I see that dress? And the madam takes it from the rails and brings it to the door. It was unthinkable that a black woman would come inside and touch a dress that a white woman would touch after her. These small things are so humiliating, such an insult to one's dignity.

One day I went into Foschini – it was just after our arrival in May '77 – I wanted something black for Zindzi to wear for 16 June.* The white saleswoman was standing in the door and as I thought she wanted to go out I pushed her aside and went in. Zindzi followed. We had seen a certain dress from outside and went to look at it. She came after us and told us to get out. We said, no, we want this dress. She said, you must stand outside! There was such a furious exchange and she said, you can go and shop in England! Normally blacks talk to the whites only in broken Afrikaans.

By the time we left there must have been a hundred people outside. Finally the police were called, but not from Brandfort, no, they came all the way from Bloemfontein. So it was a matter of security, the whole thing was a threat to state security.

*When the dead of the Soweto uprising on 16 June 1976 are commemorated.

That incident was of course the talk of town by then.

Foschini was boycotted by most blacks for a long time afterwards, and the shop suffered losses under the boycott.

Today any black can go inside and try on clothes. I can even take five or six dresses home and say, 'If my daughter doesn't like them, I'll bring them back.'

Isn't it grotesque: things that are considered normal all over the world are presented as 'political change' in South Africa. To go to the toilet – the most natural thing – is in South Africa part of the discussion on political change. When a black enters a lily-white toilet, then this is 'change'. That shows how sick our society is. But people here don't know any other way, they have no other experience. They continue to lead their blindfolded existence.

THE LOCATION

The situation in the ghetto of Brandfort is terrible – people are starving. And we can do very little to help them. Some families live in such destitute conditions, they have children and not a morsel of food in the house. As you know, our staple food is mealie-pap, this is eaten three times a day. But the majority of the community here have no morning meal, the children go to school on empty stomachs. There is only one good meal a day, that is when they come back from school and then the parents cook. During the day the lucky ones have a slice of bread. At supper-time the meal is invariably a plate of porridge and some boiled cabbage. I have lived in an urban area for many years and, of course, as a social worker was aware of the degenerating conditions we are subjected to. I personally have handled hundreds of malnutrition cases in Soweto. But it was the first time I'd seen the type of poverty I've encountered here in Brandfort. For the first time I saw with my own eyes families where the evening meal – the only meal – is comprised of mealie-pap and saline solution, ordinary salted water. They just get water from the tap or lukewarm water, put in a bit of salt and dab a piece of porridge into the water or wash the porridge down with the saline solution. It was also the first time I saw babies being fed on braised flour; they cannot afford cereal or infant food. All they do is put ordinary cake flour in a pan, braise it and, when it is a little brown, add first cold water so it doesn't lump and then hot water. They strain that and put it in a bottle. That's why we have such a high rate of gross malnutrition. The infant mortality rate is incredibly high. Almost every weekend we bury babies. Last weekend we had six funerals, this week there will be three, all children under two.

That is why it is so important to feed the children in the crèche we have built up. Every morning at seven, I collect the children under five and bring them to the church hall that we can use temporarily. In the evening at five I collect them and deliver them at home. Half of them can't even walk properly, they are so undernourished. A friendly farmer from Petersburg has given us some powdered milk and lately we have been given supplies from Operation Hunger – that helps us a lot, but actually we are living from hand to mouth.

We don't even know how to pay the women who are in charge of the crèche at the end of the month – and this is our first! We had four women trained with the help of the Methodist church, we have a hundred kids that need to be looked after and we don't even have the barest means to keep the crèche going.

We depend entirely on the charity of friends if we want to buy food for the kids. Every morning we get four loaves of bread so that the children can have a slice with their soup during the day.

For years now we have been struggling with the same problems. The miserable conditions in the township have not changed one bit. On the contrary. The health of the people is deteriorating, malnutrition is on the increase, there is no work, there are no welfare agencies where one can get some assistance for the most urgent cases. That 'clinic' up the road is just a white elephant, a dilapidated shack, manned by a nurse from the Department of Health; she has no drugs, no medicine, absolutely nothing, so that place is usually locked.

I give you an example: one of the girls I have adopted was expecting, and there were complications. So I had to go and ask for help. That nurse is a midwife and she told me there was nothing she could do. So I had to arrange for the girl to go to the hospital in Bloemfontein. But when she came back there was again no medical attention. There is no such thing here as pre- or post-natal care. That is only one case out of a population of nine thousand.

When I came here, the population was about five thousand. So it almost doubled in five years. The actual figure is probably much higher, since the unofficial numbers are not recorded in official statistics. Many people in the township don't register. Since they have no right to stay there, they are afraid they might be forced to leave. Since I have been here, not a single new house has been built. What are the people supposed to do? Without work, without a home, without money? There is no standing doctor here either. My house has been regarded as a sort of welfare station, but we cannot really give more than first aid to the many cases of kwashiorkor, diarrhoea, coughs and the inevitable stab wounds.

There are two Boer doctors who attend to their white patients first and the blacks are seen after five, and they must lie on separate couches for examination purposes. There are a few black doctors in the area, so when they pass here, they will help us. The nearest state hospital is in Bloemfontein, 55 km away. The new ambulance fee, which few people can afford, is R5 a trip.

I can't leave the magisterial district of Brandfort, and whenever we have acute cases, I have to rely on friends to drive the patients to Pelonomi hospital in Bloemfontein. So we embarked on providing mobile health facilities. But the cost of petrol and drugs eats into our funds. The Combi we received as a donation from Germany we also use to take round soup to the aged.

I used to have a huge pot of soup boiling on my stove for the schoolchildren so that they could have a warm meal during the day. Now we are trying to establish a soup kitchen at the local school with the help of enlightened schoolteachers; the principal is really a government servant and cannot be seen to be assisting me even if such a project concerns his own schoolchildren.

Many children come from the outlying farms; they walk 10 or 20 km to the local school here on empty stomachs. They leave home at three or four o'clock in the morning to be at the school at seven. That child is going to sit in the classroom until he comes out at two o'clock and then he must walk the same distance back home without a morsel of food – how can any child study like that and pass his exam? So it is necessary to have a soup kitchen at school – besides providing for the under-fives, the crèche children. The powdered soups are donations; we hope to get a stove to bake bread for the children.

We are trying to concentrate on health care. That's why we embarked on the garden project. People have realized that they can grow their own vegetables in their yard much cheaper than they can buy from the local farmers. Nobody can afford to pay 40c for a pumpkin. I gave them seeds and now they are growing spinach, onions, potatoes and carrots. Then, of course, came this terrible drought. People didn't have a drop of water and couldn't plant. More and more white farmers, who own everything here, had to leave their farms and sell them. That's how a lot of black farm workers lost their jobs and housing, and came here. That's one of our biggest problems. They come into Brandfort only to find that the administration office sends them right back to the farms. Now these people do not own land: they are the third or fourth generation, in most cases their great-grandfathers were farmhands; they know no other home, no homeland at all. They get endorsed out of Brandfort. Then they go to the Commissioner's office and the Commissioner tries to decide by their surnames with the assistance of their clerks which homeland they must go to. If they have something like a Xhosa surname, then they are told of a Transkei they have never heard of, or a Ciskei they have never heard of, or a Bophutatswana they have never heard of.

It's these labourers, the farmhands, that are most affected by the country's laws. These are the people who cannot just leave the area and look for work somewhere else. They know they have to qualify under the Pass Laws to go to the cities and they can't. And not only that, they are illiterate, unskilled labour. They normally end up being deported to the homelands.

So they stay, unregistered, and they have nothing. There are only about ten shops, three liquor stores and a few white houses in Brandfort. So how do you get jobs for nine thousand blacks?

In spite of that, people are mobilizing themselves in an attempt to become a little more viable and self-sufficient. We now have the Hector Petersen Committee (in commemoration of the first victim of the Soweto uprising), which is a body under which the crèche has been opened.

The women have started a programme which they call 'Lift up your home'. A group of nine women is involved in knitting and crocheting. Another self-help group has started to sew school uniforms full time. They are too expensive in the shops. So we sell these uniforms and the parents can pay in two or three instalments. With that money we can buy new material. A hundred metres of the original material and two sewing machines were donated to us.

There is also a Brandfort Youth Club. Quite a few are already involved in arts and crafts. We are also planning for weaving and pottery classes. Some do their own printing of material and batik.

Accommodation is always the problem. So we hope to establish a conference centre where all these self-help projects can be integrated with more welfare work, legal aid and educational courses. But that plan exists only on paper. So far there is no law against dreaming.

These initiatives, of course, cannot solve the real problem. As anywhere in the world where people are oppressed, you find a high rate of juvenile delinquency, broken families and alcoholism in the township.

Just imagine how sick this South African society is: they have these municipal beer gardens built by the white administration. So the people – destitute and desperate as they are – go there and drink. The whole thing is pathetic. The police then wait for them, parading up and down that one street in Brandfort. They wait for the people when they stagger out and dump them at the police station, especially on Fridays, so they are left there for the weekend.

On pension day you can witness a real drama. Every two months when it's pension payment here, you find over a hundred donkey carts of old people from the outlying farms coming to collect their cheques. They queue for their money as early as 4 a.m.

By three o'clock in the afternoon all cells in the police station are full of pensioners. They have been locked up because of 'drunkenness' or 'public disturbance in white Brandfort', as they call it. And the black people here don't know the laws as well as I do. They get locked up for nothing.

That's the tragedy in Brandfort: the prison is full of people like that.

The police come to me for routine checks; that has never stopped. The intimidation continues and everybody who has to do with me or my family will also be affected.

One day when they raided the house, they told me they would charge me for having spent some time in my house in Soweto.

I had been very ill – that was in November '83 – I had a serious infection in the leg and I almost died. I had called for a doctor who has helped us with our mobile clinic. He thought oral antibiotics would help, but he misjudged my condition.

Two days later Mr de Waal came, by sheer coincidence; he was then my local attorney. Somebody had sent a telegram to his address that he wanted to deliver at my house. I couldn't open the door. He found me slumped on the bed, almost unconscious. I was delirious with pain.

Zindzi was in Johannesburg, my grandchildren too. I had been too sick to look after them. Zindzi couldn't come back because they had arrested her.

Mr de Waal got such a fright when he saw me that he ran to get a local doctor. After one glance at my knee he arranged for immediate transport to the hospital. Adele, Mr de Waal's wife, rushed me to Universitas Hospital in Bloemfontein, which is white – no blacks are allowed there.

I think De Waal must have negotiated my admission with the police and the hospital, because I was in such a bad state. We got there at two o'clock. By four I still hadn't been seen by the doctor. They were probably still arguing whether a black could be operated on in that 'white' hospital. That was too much. I would rather die in the ghetto than apply for permission to be operated on in a white operating theatre. I don't want concessions. So I refused to stay. I insisted on being brought back to Brandfort in my wheelchair. I wanted to go to a clinic in Johannesburg.

The next day I was informed that the Minister had agreed that I could go on the next flight to Jo'burg. It was just in time.

The Security Police used to change shifts – they stayed in that hospital twenty-four hours a day for six weeks; they were everywhere, in the corridors, in the matron's office, even in my room.

Upon my release the doctor insisted that the leg had to be observed for ten days, so of course I wanted to stay in my house in Orlando. But the Security Police refused. They said I must go back to Brandfort and make a fresh application to come to Johannesburg after ten days.

How did they expect me to do that? I was on crutches; how could I fly to Bloemfontein or drive to Brandfort with nobody to meet me there – how on earth I could have done that, I don't know. So I did the most natural thing: I went to convalesce in my house in Orlando. The police came ceremoniously twice every day to tell me: 'Mrs Mandela, you have an hour to leave the house and go back to Brandfort.' Of course I ignored that. I was in bed for nine days. I couldn't walk. They called me out of the bedroom in my nightgown, and I would go to the sitting-room on my crutches and listen to this nonsense – I didn't even bother to reply. I could have stayed in a five-star hotel in Jo'burg, that's the alternative they offered. I ignored that too.

When I was in hospital I got a letter from Brandfort saying, sorry that I was sick and I must know that I have a lot of friends in Brandfort. When I returned, quite a few white people – some I had never talked to before – would stop me in the street or talk to me at the post office to find out what happened and wish me a speedy recovery.

They are no longer hostile. They rather enjoy the fact that their little Brandfort is on the map. I think that's what the little stolen smiles are all about. They enjoy being known to come from Brandfort, and who doesn't want to know his enemy? The nearer, the safer the place, as Mandela says. So they feel safer with me nearer them now.

Since the police threatened to charge me for staying at my house in Orlando, my relationship with them has deteriorated more than ever.

THE SECURITY POLICE

In the beginning I was kept under constant surveillance by the Security Police. When we had learned the local language, Sotho, they intensified their harassment because of our interaction with the community. 'The Soweto agitator' – the term they used before to keep the community away from us – didn't work any more. So they came for me directly.

I started being charged almost every day – so many stupid things. They all had to do with some violation of my banning order. We were in court almost every day. My house was like an 'operational area', an extension of the police station, with the Security Police going in and out.

Gert Prinsloo, the security policeman, had been especially assigned to watch all my movements. He was over-zealous in trying to catch me redhanded violating my banning order. During the first year, Prinsloo often came in the middle of the night to look under the bed and under the cupboard, just to check if there were any forbidden visitors. We had such rows that he has been keeping more distance lately – now he parks himself up on a hill with binoculars.

I have been banned since 1962. The last banning order, which of course included house arrest every night and at weekends – the one that was served on me on 16 May 1977, the day I was exiled here – I think I left on the desk in Protea police station. There is no longer any need for me to read that type of document. It has been my way of life and the way of life of all those who have been similarly banned. I know it by heart.

This one now is under the Internal Security Act.* It hardly makes a difference. All the other years I was banned under the Suppression of Communism Act. This one is a little more stringent than the other. That's the only difference really. It's exactly the same document I got in 1962. But, as I say, a little more stringent as the years go by. It has conformed to the pattern of the racist regime, stripping us of each and every human right. It is detestable, abhorrent and only of relevance in so far as I have to comply with it, but I can't waste my time and bother to read that damned document any more.

I can't even go to church without a permit. But I will never go and ask a magistrate if I can go and worship God. That's going too far, giving them the religious powers they think they have. That would be accepting that their powers superseded those of God. I will never ask for permission from a human being to go to church. That is God's right and nobody else's.

There are about ten churches for this small community here – that's all they have in abundance, huge structures; the most modern is the Dutch Reformed Church. There are no multiracial churches; there is an Anglican church for blacks, but there is no priest. So a friend of our family, Father John Rushton from the Anglican church, has come once a week to give me Holy Communion.

He was not allowed in my house. Only the doctor and the lawyer were allowed to enter – apart from my children. So when he got there,

---

*The Suppression of Communism Act, 1950, one of the numerous draconian laws for the oppression of political opponents, was replaced by the Internal Security Act of 1976, under which the same – though more stringent – regulations apply. It prohibits any act (or omission) which is calculated to advocate, defend or encourage any of the objects of communism (Marxist socialism); any act which aims at any political, industrial, social or economic change in South Africa by the promotion of disturbance or disorder with the ultimate purpose of establishing a communist system of government. The Act of 1976 stipulates that any activities are prohibited which endanger or are calculated to endanger the security of the state or the maintenance of public order. The Minister of Justice decides which activities can be seen as furthering any of the objects of communism or endangering the security of the state. The law allows for preventive detention without trial, without access to a court of law, and gives power to the executive to silence any organization, any individual or the Press.

he hooted outside my cells – that's what the house is, just a combination of three cells put together – and I ran out and we prayed outside his car, giving me Holy Communion on the bonnet; and when it rained we sat inside the car.

The Security Police – when we went to the christening of my grandchild in the cathedral in Bloemfontein – who do you think was leaning against the wall, observing the whole sermon? Prinsloo! He even mingled with us, the close relatives!

I felt so ashamed of our white South Africans. They seemed to see nothing wrong with that, it was normal for them. Such gross infringements become so much part of their life that they see nothing wrong with it! 'Where there are these terrorists, there must be police, even in the house of God!'

Then there was another incident which shows how abnormally they react to normal human behaviour: friends, Helen Joseph and Barbara Whaite, used to bring me some food – that was early in 1977. Father Rakale usually brought them and notified me of their arrival. This time he couldn't come, so they sent me a telegram from the post office and I rushed to town. There were warm exchanges and I was careful to greet one at a time. I parked a few yards away from them. We took the groceries from Barbara's car to mine. It started raining. So Barbara was sitting in the back of the car, Helen Joseph in front. I stood next to the car and spoke to Barbara. After a few minutes Gert emerged with a shroud of leaves around his face – he had been watching from behind the fence. He had been sitting in the hedge, his head dripping with water. It was the usual thing: 'I've caught you violating your order and I'm placing you under arrest.'

There was a court case against Helen and Barbara. They had to spend four months in jail because they refused to give evidence.

I've had encounters with that man almost every day here. When he heard that I had spoken to someone he would round up the whole street and interrogate them. When I was in a certain house, he would pick up the father, mother, child and grandparents, and interrogate them. There must be volumes and volumes of statements in the police station.

Once Helen Suzman* came to visit. When she arrived, the police

---

*Helen Suzman: Member of Parliament since 1952; from 1961 to 1974 the only MP of the opposition party (now the Progressive Federal Party); one of the best-known critics of the apartheid system.

were busy raiding my house. She 'welcomed' the 'reception committee', and while the police confiscated books and documents – they even took the bedspread because it had the colours of the ANC* – we just sat and chatted (they had to walk around us) and didn't pay any attention to them.

Prinsloo always knew what I was doing. There are informers everywhere, that's just a way of life here. There are too many people with empty stomachs who have nothing to lose.

They informed Prinsloo about my visitors just to survive. They still do; the only difference is that they will now inform with a conscience. Some came to me and apologized: they even told me how much they got: 50c. I felt so insulted. I actually told him one day: 'How dare you underpay my people! How dare you think I'm worth 50c to them – that's two bottles of beer!' He simply blushed pepper-red.

When Helen came she often brought me food, and I used to give some to the kids. So what did Gert do? He went to every child that got an orange, he went to the school and forced the principal to explain to the parents in a public meeting that it was prohibited for the children to accept fruit or any other presents from a 'communist'.

There was another court case. I had been two weeks in Brandfort and it was very cold. Prinsloo had brought an old coal farm stove (that Caledon Dover type) and a bag of coal – which I had to pay for. With two pieces that stove was full and it wouldn't burn. I met a woman who showed sympathy and I wanted to ask her where to get small coal nuts. I used to have friendly chats with her and she would give me household tips on how to keep the dust out of the house by putting wet rags or newspaper in the cracks of the walls and between the window frames. I used to spend three quarters of my whole day trying to disinfect and clean that house. Just as I was there, the postman came to her house with eggs, vegetables and a chicken and he said: 'Look, the chicken from the farmer at the post office is very good today, we can place an order.' (Farmers come on certain days and sell groceries at the post office.) I asked him how much he paid for it – and was charged with breaking my bans.

*Twenty-six leading members of the American Congress sent Mrs Mandela a replacement bedspread, in a Pennsylvania Dutch design which is supposed to keep evil spirits away.

As a banned person I am forbidden to talk to more than one person, but of course that was not a 'social gathering' but an accidental meeting and I was later acquitted on appeal.

Where else in the world can the question of the price of a chicken be interpreted as 'furthering the aims of communism'?

For Gert, even saying 'hello' to a person in the street is forbidden. I had to educate him about their banning orders. When Prinsloo came to charge me because I had received my own family, I had to tell him that he doesn't even know their laws.

The laws they make get so intricate that they no longer know what they are doing. No wonder: if you spend twenty-four hours of the day legislating against twenty-two million people, how can your mind be clear on anything. It must be totally entangled in this network of racial laws.

M. K. Malefane, a young artist and friend of the family, was also constantly harassed. They wanted to get him out of Brandfort and even deported him to the Transkei.

One day they came in paramilitary attire, boasting they had just returned from 'mowing down terrorists in Lesotho' and now they were coming to kill us. They put him in a sort of cage where he had to cower and couldn't move.

Their argument was that his stay in my house was illegal. But my banning order doesn't include my household. I was never asked what my household consisted of. M. K. was part of that household and shouldn't be affected by my banning order. On the basis of that, the case was thrown out of court.

Of course none of us have legal papers for Brandfort. My legal rights are in Johannesburg, so are Zindzi's and M. K.'s. I don't belong in the Free State. Under influx control, which is of their own making, I'm a legal resident of Johannesburg. So we can't even go to Bloemfontein. Whenever we go there, we get detained and our lawyer has to get us out. There is a whole string of cases.

In the early years of our exile, Zindzi wanted to go away and couldn't understand why I didn't let her go. I needed her physically. She is my youngest. I have given up everything to the cause – without any regrets of course – but at the same time you do want a sense of belonging, you do need a home. Because you are committed, it doesn't mean you don't want a home. I literally couldn't let her out of my clutches, clinging to perhaps the last semblance of a family unit. Deep inside she felt torn apart: did she have to leave me in the *backveld* of the Free State, in this kind of insecurity and in danger – with a home locked up in Johannesburg? And there was also her father in jail.

She is over that crisis now. The one thing she has always wanted to do is law. I think being the type of child she is, that would be the best profession for her. Definitely she will be a political lawyer.

THE DE WAALS

I have great respect for Piet de Waal.* He and his family went through a lot because he was my attorney. He even fell out with Jimmy Kruger, then the Minister of so-called Justice, because he was acting for me. Kruger said to him, 'Why don't you let her find a Jewish lawyer – what the hell forces you to act for that woman!'

Of course at first De Waal was nervous, but he couldn't refuse me as a client. It was a question of the professional ethics of the Law Society – and also he was the only attorney in Brandfort.

Before my arrival he hardly ever had dealings with the police, but afterwards he continually had to get me out of prison, he had to defend me in court. As a result of that, they were ostracized by the white community – we were directly responsible for that.

After all, he lives with these people, they play golf together. I cannot put my appreciation into words – we really became the best of friends.

He has changed a lot since I first met him. When I think back to our first meeting in his office on Voortrekker Road in May 1977! That shock on the face of his secretary when I arrived! I am sure I was the first black client who didn't come through the back door. She didn't know what to do with me. She must have been too embarrassed to offer me a seat, so she instantly called Mr de Waal, even though he was busy with a client. He was so shaken. He was holding a pen in his hand and the pen dropped.

Adele, his wife, was totally different. She introduced herself and said, 'You must be terribly lonely in a place like this. Please come over to my house at any time – I'm sure you would like some books to read.'

*Until fairly recently, Piet de Waal was Winnie Mandela's local attorney.

That was the first humane attitude I got in white Brandfort; she was the first to behave like that. She quickly prepared warm meals for Zindzi and I to take home when we didn't have anywhere to cook. From then on, she always extended invitations, she wanted to teach me knitting or dressmaking.

I have learned a lot from her, a lot I could never have learned otherwise. Living with her these past years and so close to her, as an Afrikaner woman in the Free State, I've understood their problems.

One day she sent an urgent message for me, I must come over. So I go to her house and I find her aged parents there. And she introduces me to them. I could see the expression on their faces! We had problems, of course, communicating, because they are from one of the *backveld* little *dorps* in the Free State – proper, proper Afrikaners. So we struggle along. I don't know Afrikaans. I don't know a word up to now – I've developed a psychological wall against it – I cannot even greet someone in Afrikaans!

We had a lovely afternoon together. Just before I left, both of them stood up and you could see, there was a rehearsed little statement and they stood next to each other and the old man spoke and said, 'Mrs Mandela, we want to tell you that we bear you no grudge.'

I nearly dropped down. I would have thought it should be the other way round! And the innocence with which they said it; it was so sweet: 'They bear me no grudge.' I have wronged them. What a statement to make! It summarized the whole Afrikaner outlook. And, honestly, that is the problem of the white man in this country. It was a very serious statement. We are virtually at war. I should feel guilty because, by virtue of my blackness – not even my political views – I have wronged them.

Here I am, I am twenty-two million – it's not the right thing to say to them, because they didn't mean it that way and yet, at the same time, they did really mean it that way. Here is a settler, telling me in my country, when I'm trying to get it back, that he bears me no grudge. I was stunned.

As a result of our friendship, Adele was ostracized by the white community. All her friends stayed away. Any time you'd come to her house, you'd find her alone, doing her needlework and tapestry. And that hurt me terribly.

There were also difficulties with her daughter Sonia. She would hardly eat any more. I think we were indirectly responsible for her illness – it lasted two years. When she met a girl like Zindzi, who was almost her age, and they had this tremendous exchange of ideas, it was somewhat of a traumatic shock for the little Afrikaner girl from the *backveld* of the Free State. She honestly never knew. And then Zindzi always talked about her school, Waterford, this multiracial school in Swaziland. And Sonia started nagging her parents about letting her go to Waterford. Goodness me, a step like that, for an Afrikaner from the Free State! It became very difficult for Adele to handle this. That Calvinistic Afrikaner background – it's not that easy to break away from it.

The De Waal family has been very brave. For Piet de Waal, our talks and the first encounter with blacks other than his farmhands were an eye-opener. He even told me that we are doing exactly the same as his forefathers, when they were trying to get their country back from the Englishman.

Their outlook has totally changed. They suddenly realize that a man like Nelson should never have been jailed in the first place. Now he sees that the same man in fact is fighting for them. They never knew that these so-called communists are people who want to live with them, people who want to accommodate them, people who accept the reality of their existence, people who are prepared to recognize the fact that they have built the country as much as everybody else has and that their role should be recognized by future governments. These people should never have been prosecuted. And yet, these are the very same people the government wants to get rid of. Then what kind of society does the government want – if they do not even accept our Freedom Charter? What kind of unreal society is it, which has already produced such tragic results that history can never wipe out?

The dilemma of that type of Afrikaner is far bigger than mine. I have no problem with my liberation – I know what I want. He – in his position, with his neurotic obsession with his preservation and this obsessive fear of being dominated – he has worse problems than anybody else.

But when a descendant of Piet Retief – a Piet in Brandfort – and a descendant of Shaka and Dingaan – a Mandela – start to get to know and like each other and to think that their future can only be a common one, maybe this is a sign of hope.

EXTRACT FROM LETTER FROM NELSON MANDELA TO WINNIE MANDELA

1.7.79

My darling Mum,

Your letters of 12 May and 24 May arrived on the same day. I have already sent you a medical report in my last letter and I don't think the doctor will give you anything new. I must once again assure you that I feel quite well and alert ...

I really agree with the advice that we should close the files with Mr de Waal and deal directly with Johannesburg. But in doing so, you must write [him] a formal letter of thanks. It has been courageous of Mr de Waal in such a small and isolated community to attend to our affairs. The incitement he received from certain quarters as to how he should treat us is just one illustration. His association with the family marks him out and his wife as a family of deep conviction and strength of character.

EXTRACT FROM LETTER FROM WINNIE MANDELA TO MARY BENSON*

24.5.79

Well, since miracles don't stop happening the first thing I'll do when I'm unbanned (if I ever am) is to go to church to thank God for letting your letter reach me via Gert Prinsloo at a time when I was thinking of all our dear friends and taking stock of myself, a common feature of exile. Being with Zindzi in the past two years sort of cushioned the impact of the pain; now she is gone to prepare for exams and is with Helen. It is the first time that I truly feel what my little Siberia is all about. The empty long days drag on, one like the other, no matter how hard I try to study. The solitude is deadly, the grey matchbox shacks so desolate simply stare at you as lifeless as the occupants, who form a human chain of frustration as they pass next to my window; from the moment the bar opens until it closes at 8 p.m., they are paralytic drunk; schoolchildren who find nothing

---

* An old-time friend of the Mandela family, born in South Africa. She was banned for her political involvement, and now works as a writer and lobbyist in England. Her books include a life of Nelson Mandela and a history of the African National Congress.

to eat at home when they return from pseudo-schools simply join their parents there. They haven't even the 'honour' of being sojourners in this ghetto, they are spare labour units of the fat farmers who threw them out of their farms in the first place. The highest wage is R5 a month for the lucky mothers. Social life is the nightly raids and funerals!

How grim that must sound, yet there's something so purifying about exile, each minute is a reminder that blackness alone is a commitment in our sick society; it is so strengthening too, I have no doubt how sacrosanct our cause is and how near we are to our goal in terms of historical periods. What could be greater than being part of such a cause no matter how infinitesimal our contribution is.

By the way, I was due to start work on 1 March 1979 for a Dr Chris Hattingh in Welkom, who was a great sympathizer and a fanatical admirer of Nelson's. He was one of them, the Afrikaners. He maintained us financially for a few months. I battled to get permission to work for him from October last year. Brig. Coetzee told me permission was granted and I could start but had to wait for it in writing. In the meantime he [Hattingh] told me he was being trailed by a car with four men since he had been visiting us. On 1 March the day I should have started work, he came to find out about the permit; six kilometres from me, at 8 p.m., his car mysteriously overturned and he died on the spot. After his death, permission was promptly granted in writing. They killed him and have got away with it – like the Steve Bikos, but this one is worse as the world will never know. I haven't got over the shock yet and I never knew I could grieve so much for someone other than my own kind. In a way it's taught me a deeper depth of love which might have been superficial and ideological, now it's real and honest for those who identify so completely with us.

Will be seeing Nelson on 2 June. I learn that the latest book marking his sixtieth birthday is terrific.

When My Father Taught Me
History I Began to Understand

GROWING UP IN THE COUNTRYSIDE (PONDOLAND)

'I became aware at an early stage that the whites felt superior to us. And I could see how shabby my father looked in comparison to the white teachers. That hurts your pride when you are a child; you tell yourself: "If they failed in those nine Xhosa wars, I am one of them, and I will start from where those Xhosas left off and get my land back."'

The part of Pondoland where I come from is still totally tribal; tribesmen still congregate on the hills, wearing their traditional blankets. I went to a country school and my political enlightenment was very vague at that stage.

My father was a history teacher in the government service; he was supposed to be some little tribal chief, but he refused to take up that position (which I couldn't understand at that time). It was only in the classroom that I learned about the background of my country.

My mother, a domestic science teacher, was a religious fanatic. When I was only eight years old we used to get locked up in a room with her and my little sister, and she forced us to pray aloud. When my father was there, she would take us – two or three times a day – to a corner in the garden. It had high grass and formed some kind of protective shelter and she would pray. We had to follow her in these religious rituals, which we didn't understand. This has always been so ingrained that my own rebellion against the Church later, in high school, I think was a rebellion against that kind of petticoat government from her. In all her prayers she prayed for her children. She must have been crazy for

46

a boy. I remember her asking God every day for a son. This also developed in me the feeling, I will prove to her that a girl is as much of value to a parent as a son. Also, my belief in God had been shaken in my childhood, when mother, who prayed three times a day for my gravely ill sister, one Sunday returned from church and found 'Sisi Vuyelwa' coughing blood – bleeding to death. I was standing behind my father, a little girl of seven, when he pulled a white sheet over my sister whilst mother knelt in a starched white petticoat next to her bed, exhorting God to send his angels to save my sister. She must have had TB.

From then on, mother was never the same. I watched her wither away, sitting in the dark corners of the house and praying silently. I think she could have had cancer. She lay there, just diminishing daily; for me as a little girl, she was literally disappearing, and she was in great pain, that's all I remember. She had probably had too many children for her age – we were nine – and she must have been about forty when she died.

As I watched her lips move and her tear-drenched face, I hated that God who didn't respond to her and who instead came for her when she was breastfeeding a three-month baby boy – my brother Thanduxolo. I battled to prepare his feeding bottles for him at the age of nine and spent hours at night cuddling him and trying to put him to sleep with sugared water.

We had to find our way in life after mother's death, disciplined by my father's sisters, who were ruthless and hard. Children had to be taught the hardships of life!

When my mother died, I had to leave school for half a year to work in the fields; I milked cows and looked after our own sheep and goat, and I had to harvest the crops, our mealies – that's where the bulk of the muscles comes from. It was a miracle that I passed Standard 6.

Father battled to keep the family of nine children well fed with a putrid teacher's salary that hardly differentiated him from the rural peasants, my people, who lived from the sweat of their brows, tilling the arid land with no farming tools but the crude plough and with emaciated cattle which I took to the 'dipping tank', where the white man tried to kill the ticks for the tribesmen.

When my father taught me history, I began to understand. I remember distinctly, for instance, how he taught us about the nine

47

Xhosa wars. Of course we had textbooks, naturally written by white men, and they had *their* interpretation, why there were nine 'Kaffir' wars. Then he would put the textbook aside and say: 'Now, this is what the book says, but the truth is: these white people invaded our country and stole the land from our grandfathers. The clashes between white and black were originally the result of cattle thefts. The whites took the cattle and the blacks would go and fetch them back.' That's how he taught us our history.

And then he would say, for example, 'Adam Kok, whom they refer to as a Hottentot, he was one of our leaders. His people were perhaps more robbed than any other little tribe in the area. They went so far as to exchange cattle with table knives!' And my father warned us: 'When your fathers go to the mines, they will be regarded as "boys", even by the white children, and when your mothers go to town to work for your education, they will be called "girls". It's a white man's way of insulting a black man.'

At least during that time there was not yet a difference between white and black education. It was before the rubbish Bantu education was brought in in the early fifties. There was a common syllabus and we were doing academic subjects like Latin, English, chemistry, physics and mathematics. There were strict standards. With the introduction of Bantu education standards dropped, the horizon became narrow and provincial. We still learnt about America and China. The children who came after us learn the distance from Brandfort to Bloemfontein and what they grow in the homelands. They know nothing about the world and can't even speak English properly.

So I became aware at an early age that the whites felt superior to us. And I could see how shabby my father looked in comparison to the white teachers. That hurts your pride when you are a child; you tell yourself: 'If they failed in those nine Xhosa wars, I am one of them and I will start from where those Xhosas left off and get my land back.'

Every tribal child felt that way. That was the result of my father's lessons in the classroom.

There is an anger that wakes up in you when you are a child and it builds up and determines the political consciousness of the black man.

There was a song, for instance, the Bloemfontein song, which we used to sing – my father taught us music too – and I still remember its beginning: 'When our black leaders came together in Bloemfontein,* there was a big *indaba* and the leaders called upon the black people to unite and fight the common enemy.'

My father taught us other songs which dealt with events in the history of our people. They were songs from the tribesmen, by traditional composers.

And my brothers at home sang the songs they had learned from the elders up in the mountains of Pondoland, where I come from. They were songs about the mineworkers: how the men feel about having to leave their homes and their children, when they go far away to work as contract workers for the white man.

I still know the words today. The white makes a mistake, thinking the tribal black is docile and subservient.

When I went to Shawbury High School, I saw the white toddlers in town wearing beautiful dresses. We were nine in our family, my father could never afford to clothe us all. The white kids had buses to school; we had to walk barefoot many miles a day. I wore shoes for the first time in secondary school, and that was only because it was part of the school uniform. I never even questioned whether we could afford shoes or other things.

There was one teacher I loved very much. He had his own way of teaching us about our struggle and he idolized Bismarck. We had a long corridor and before he came to our class, he started at the far end, shouting: 'The unification of Germany, Bismarck believed, could not be attained through parliamentary speeches and debates, but by means of bl-o-o-o-d and iron.' By the time he said "bl-o-o-o-d' he had reached our classroom. It was so funny. And he continued: 'And so is our struggle in this country.' He was so obsessed with it, that there was not a single examination paper which didn't have that and all of us sang that quotation. That is how I came to believe that my own struggle is to be won by means of blood and iron. (*Laughs*).

By the way, my father always had the greatest admiration for the German people and their industrial achievements. That's why he insisted on that terrible name 'Winifred', which subsequently became 'Winnie'. He also believed in the Christian names, because of the missionaries. Whenever he disciplined us he would refer to the hard-

---

*The conference which founded the African National Congress in 1912.

49

working and industrious Germans. He wanted us to become as strong as they are. As if I had my fighting spirit from them!

But since I became internationally known under that name, I'll have to continue with it. After all, it is a constant reminder of our oppression! My African name 'Nomzamo' means in Xhosa 'trial' – those who in their life will go through many trials – also in the sense of court trials . . .

In high school we came for the first time into contact with political debate. Some of our teachers belonged to what was formerly called the 'Society of Young Africa', the so-called Conventionists. They were very theoretical, and tended to be apart from the masses. It was a scholastic political organization, terribly aloof from the people, the proletariat. We admired them – at that time we didn't have contact with any other political organization.

Then in 1952 we heard of the Defiance Campaign, when thousands of people all over the country refused to obey some of the race laws.

I was in my final year of matric, and the students in the rural set-up didn't understand what was happening. They were politicized, but did not know exactly what the Defiance Campaign meant nationwide. They heard 'defiance', so they defied authority in school, they defied us, the prefects. 'Away with authority' was their slogan, and the school nearly closed down. Very few took exams. We were taking our final exams, but the rest of the school followed the boycott.

So when I came to Johannesburg in 1953, the meetings I attended as a first-year student in social work were those of the Convention. We used to attend them in dilapidated buildings in Doornfontein – we were not allowed to participate openly in politics as students. We knew of Nelson Mandela as a patron of our school. The motto of the school of social work was 'Know thyself', and the students associated that concept with his name. The students in the urban area were much better versed in the political thinking of the day.

The hostel where I lived, in Jeppe Street, was comprised of ordinary workers, and I think 95 per cent of those workers belonged to the African National Congress. I came into contact with slogans and literature of the ANC at that hostel.

There were also girls who belonged to the various trade union movements and brought pamphlets and document along from their meetings and we found ourselves discussing political issues all the time.

They would invariably talk about this Mandela, Tambo and Nokwe – just about the whole leadership of the ANC – and above all, the president of the African National Congress, Chief Lutuli.

At the same hostel was Adelaide Tsukudu, who was later to marry Oliver Tambo. She was a staff nurse at the general hospital. She took me around Johannesburg – I was new in town and the only student from the rural area in the whole school. She was very much in love with Oliver Tambo at the time, and I would go with her when she was meeting him, and sometimes we would get a lift from him. That was the beginning of my political education as far as the ANC was concerned. From the hostel I found myself drifting to the African National Congress. I went along with these girls, who used to attend the huge meetings at Trades Hall. That's where the workers were, the people we were dealing with as junior social workers. That was the beginning of my contact with SACTU, the South African Congress of Trade Unions. After my graduation in social work I worked at Baragwanath Hospital – that was in December 1955.

It as soon after that I met Nelson Mandela.

NOMAWETHU MBERE, A SCHOOLFRIEND, REMEMBERS

We went to Shawbury High School at the outskirts of the Transkei. We had to go to the church service four times a day – the first one would start at 6 a.m. Winnie would take a lead in organizing the services.

She was elected chief-prefect for the supervision of all the girls from forms one to five. At that time she was very reserved and introvert but her leadership was to be seen early. We had these debating clubs and the way she disciplined the students and kept them together was remarkable. She had very good marks and she loved sports, she was very good at netball. She used to win trophies at the sports festival in Umtata.

Winnie was two classes ahead and she used to help me and the other girls in our assignments; so much so that at one time when I was able to explain the difference between export and import in class, my teacher admonished me that I wasn't supposed to know that as yet. I was too advanced in the curriculum!

She used to share everything. I had nothing and she had a bit of pocket-money. So she would buy cream for 5c and share that cream with me for three weeks, until her father sent her some more. We used to exchange shirts and dresses and wear them alternately so as to hide that we only had one school uniform each.'

THE YOUNG SOCIAL WORKER – DR NTHATHO MOTLANA

Dr Nthatho Motlana, the Mandelas' family doctor now for thirty-five years and a leading political figure in Soweto, remembers Winnie Mandela as a young girl:

I've known her since she was nineteen. She had just qualified in social work and had come to do clinical training in Baragwanath Hospital.

Winnie has always been interested in people, she has always had a highly developed social conscience. She has always gone out of her way to help people and I am not saying that because she is a friend or a political colleague. It's unbelievable the kind of things she'll do – spending money from her own pocket, which wasn't much. You would find her touring the townships, looking for destitute old ladies with nobody to look after them, waking me up in the middle of the night to say, there is that lady in such and such a place, who needs medical treatment; just ordinary people. At nineteen, as early as that! She worries so much about people, much more than about herself.

THE YOUNG SOCIAL WORKER – A COLLEAGUE

One of Winnie's colleagues at the hospital remembers her in those days:

The difference from other girls was striking. Here was a young social worker who would really stand up for other people. It was also remarkable that her table was always full of books on politics and economics. But even then she could be very firm. There was an incident when Dr Motlana had diagnosed pellagra in a patient, and he was to get sick-leave for three weeks. As a social worker, Winnie had to justify that decision towards the patient's bosses, who were angry about the loss of labour. The letter that she wrote – you should have read that! 'You have to accept my competence. The decision stands!' The patient got his three weeks' sick-leave.

NELSON MANDELA AND THE AFRICAN NATIONAL CONGRESS

Nelson Rolihlahla Mandela had come to Johannesburg from the Transkei in 1941. Born in Umtata on 18 July 1918, one of the royal family of the Tembu, he had an inbred sense of responsibility. His had been a traditional pastoral childhood – he herded sheep and helped with the ploughing and, as he recalled in a statement to the court when he was on trial in 1962, he was stirred by stories that elders of the tribe told about the days before the coming of the white man:

> Then our people lived peacefully, under the democratic rule of
> their kings ... Then the country was ours, in our own name and
> right. The land belonged to the whole tribes. There were no classes,
> no rich or poor and no exploitation of man by man. All men were
> free and equal and this was the foundation of government. The
> council was so completely democratic that all members of the tribe
> could participate in its deliberations. Chief and subject, warrior
> and medicine man, all took part and endeavoured to influence its
> decisions. There was much in such a society that was primitive and
> insecure, and certainly could never measure up to the demands of
> the present epoch. But in such a society are contained the seeds of
> revolutionary democracy, in which none will be held in slavery or
> servitude, and in which poverty, want and insecurity shall be no
> more. This is the inspiration which, even today, inspires me and
> my comrades in our political struggle.

He was to meet many of those comrades in Johannesburg. Cutting short his education – he had been suspended from Fort Hare college for taking part in student protests – he was among the tens of thousands who flocked to the city in the wartime industrial boom. He found that poverty, overcrowding and constant harassment by police was the lot of most 'Natives' in the teeming locations and shanty-towns to which they were confined. His political education had begun and was stimulated by a new friend, Walter

Sisulu – several years older, self-educated and widely experienced after working in the gold mines, as a servant and as a factory hand.

Sisulu introduced him to the African National Congress at much the same time as a fellow-student from Fort Hare joined the organization: Oliver Tambo, also newly arrived in Johannesburg to teach at St Peter's, the school for Africans established by Father Trevor Huddleston's order, the Community of the Resurrection. Founded in 1912, even before Afrikaner Nationalists had set up their party, the ANC was imbued with humanitarian ideals, peacefully agitating for removal of the colour bar; its methods – deputations, petitions, protest meetings – provoked the three young men, along with Anton Lembede, Peter Mda and other African Nationalists, into forming a Youth League in 1944, to 'galvanize' the movement. Against a background of social and industrial ferment, night after night they met to discuss, argue and plan.

In 1948 the Afrikaner Nationalists came to power with their policy of apartheid. Ever more draconian laws would separate and subjugate the so-called 'non-white' majority: forced removals under the Group Areas Act; restriction of movement and break-up of families under the Urban Areas Act; skilled jobs reserved for whites; inferior education imposed on the 'Bantu'; and the 'Bantu' four-fifths of the population – apart from a necessary labour force – eventually to be relegated to 'homelands' occupying 13 per cent of South Africa. Mandela described it as a grim programme of mass evictions, political persecution and police terror.

Thus through institutionalized violence, the white minority of this heavily armed and policed state intended to maintain power, wealth and privilege.

The Youth League had formulated a Programme of Action, specifically non-violent, which inspired the Defiance Campaign of 1952. Mandela was elected joint Volunteer-in-Chief with Maulvi Cachalia, whose father had supported Gandhi when he initiated passive resistance in South Africa in 1907. In a surge of protest against selected unjust laws, men and women all over the country – Africans, Indians and a handful of whites – courted imprisonment, challenging the pass laws and colour-bar regulations. In all, 8,500 went to jail before exceptionally severe legislation finally halted this activity.

Mandela was one of twenty leaders convicted for organizing the campaign. In giving them nine-month suspended sentences, the Judge made the significant remark that the 'statutory communism' of which they had been found guilty, 'had nothing to do with communism as it is commonly known'.

And he accepted evidence that they had consistently advised their followers to maintain 'a peaceful course of action and to avoid violence in any shape or form'. Nevertheless, the government proceeded to ban one after another of the leaders and organizers under the Suppression of Communism Act. In the years to come the ANC's capacity to survive would be tested; new methods of carrying on must continually be devised; yet the movement would never be crushed. Shortly after Mandela was elected to the important role of President of the Transvaal Congress, he was prohibited from attending gatherings and confined to Johannesburg. A year later he was ordered to resign from the organization and all related bodies. His public voice might be silenced, but he worked on behind the scenes.

Meanwhile, encouraged by Sisulu, he had qualified as an attorney and, in partnership with Oliver Tambo, who had abandoned teaching, had set up a practice near the law courts, resisting official orders to remove their firm to a township. To their office flocked victims of the system: delegations of peasants ejected from land they had occupied for generations; husbands and wives whose life together was 'illegal'. Each case in court, each visit to the jails, gave evidence of apartheid's brutality: 'The whole life of any thinking African,' Mandela was to say when on trial in 1962, 'drives him continuously to a conflict between his conscience on the one hand and the law on the other ... a law which, in our view, is immoral, unjust and intolerable ... We must protest against it, we must oppose it, we must attempt to alter it.'

He now found himself professionally at risk: the Transvaal Law Society petitioned the Supreme Court to have him struck off the roll for the Defiance Campaign conviction. But the court upheld his case: there was nothing dishonourable, its findings stated, in a lawyer identifying himself with his people in their struggle for human rights, even if his activities infringed the laws.

Mandela had married some years earlier and lived with his wife, Evelyn Ntoko, and three children, Thembi, Makgatho and Pumla, in a small block house in Orlando, near Walter and Albertina Sisulu. During the mid fifties the marriage broke up. He continued to live in the house alone, working on a series of articles, involved in plans for the Congress of the People, and in working out methods for strengthening the ANC at grass-roots level.

The historic Congress of the People on 26 June 1955 at Kliptown, outside Johannesburg, was the brainchild of the distinguished academic, Professor Z. K. Matthews. Many leaders were prevented from attending by banning orders – among them the President-General of the ANC, Chief Albert Lutuli, Walter Sisulu, who had been Secretary-General, and Mandela; but 3,000 people of all races adopted a Freedom Charter which defined a future South Africa. It began: 'South Africa belongs to all who live in it, black and white.'*

The Charter became the policy of a Congress Alliance in which the ANC was joined by the SA Indian Congress, the Coloured People's Congress, the SA Congress of Trade Unions and the white Congress of Democrats.

In December 1956 Mandela was one of 156 men and women of all races arrested on charges of treason. Many were leaders such as Lutuli and Matthews, Tambo and Sisulu, but many had been minor organizers of the Congress of the People. The essence of the case, as the State put it, was the belief that the liberation movement was part of an international communist-inspired effort pledged to overthrow the government by violence. Four and a half years would be spent in attempting to prove this: the Freedom Charter and the Youth League's 1949 Programme of Action were key documents.

The preliminary hearing opened in the Johannesburg Drill Hall. Oliver Tambo was among those released in the early stages; Mandela remained on trial and, through weekends and during adjournments, carried on his practice.

It was during a break in the trial that he met Winnie Madikizela.

*See Appendix.

Life with Him Was Always a Life without Him

MEETING NELSON MANDELA

'We never had him physically to share that love he exudes so much of. I knew when I married him that I married the struggle, the liberation of my people.'

I saw Nelson Mandela for the first time in the Johannesburg Regional Court. He was representing a colleague of mine who had been assaulted by police. I just saw this towering, imposing man, actually quite awesome. (*Giggles.*) As he walked into court, the crowd whispered his name. He doesn't even know about this incident.

The second time was in the company of Oliver Tambo and Adelaide Tsukudu (later his wife). Oliver comes from Bizana, the same village I come from, so I knew him slightly, and Adelaide and I were living at a hostel, the Helping Hand Club, and were close friends. I had just got off the bus from Baragwanath Hospital and they drove by and offered me a lift. Adelaide said she was starving so we stopped at a delicatessen. Oliver found he had no money but they noticed Nelson in the shop and Oliver said, 'Tell him to pay.' Which he did, and when he came out with Adelaide, Oliver introduced me as 'Winnie from Bizana'.

Soon after, I got a telephone call from Nelson. He invited me to lunch and said he would send a friend to fetch me. I was of course petrified – he was much older than me and he was a patron of my school of social work. We had never seen him, he was just a name on the letterheads; he was too important for us students to even know him. So when I got this call, I couldn't work for the rest of the day. And when I prepared to go and meet him, I took out every schoolgirl's dress I possessed. Nothing seemed suitable – in those days we had almost knee-length frilled dresses that made one look even younger and more ridiculous. And when I ultimately found something more dignified – it wasn't even mine. I felt so uncomfortable.

It was a Sunday. He always worked right through – Saturdays, Sundays, Mondays, the days were the same. I was driven to his office where he was buried in files, there were stacks and stacks of files all over, and it was just about lunch-time.

We went to an Indian restaurant. I tasted Indian food for the first time – a little country bumpkin from Pondoland. I had associated most of the time with my professional colleagues and I hadn't really known much about Johannesburg social life. It was such a struggle to eat. I couldn't swallow. I was almost in tears because of this hot, hot curry. And he noticed and embarrassingly gave me a glass of water and said, 'If you find it too hot, it helps to take a sip of water.' And he was enjoying that hot unbearable food!

As we were eating, he couldn't swallow one spoonful without people coming to consult him – it was an impossible set-up. It went right through that very first appointment. And I felt so left out, I just didn't fit in.

Leaving the restaurant, going to his car, we took something like half an hour. Nelson couldn't walk from here to there without having consultations. He is that type of person, almost impossible to live with as far as the public is concerned.

He belongs to them. I didn't know that that was to be the pace of my life. I was just stunned and fascinated.

When we got back to the office it was the same story – there were people everywhere. So we drove out of town and walked in the veld, and he told me he had in fact phoned to ask if I could help raise funds for the Treason Trial. He never even asked me what my political affiliations were or whether I had any views at all. And I never dreamt of asking: how do I fit in, in this whole complex structure?

When we were walking back to the car, the path was rocky and my sandal strap broke. I was walking with difficulty, barefoot, so he held my hand as my father would hold a little girl's hand, and just before we got in the car, he said, 'It was a lovely day,' and just turned and kissed me.

The following day I got a phone call to say I would be picked up when I knocked off from work. He was there in the car dressed in his gym attire. He was a fanatic from the fitness point of view, so he was in his training clothes. That's where I was taken, to the gym, to watch him sweat out!

That was the pattern of my life right through the week. I was picked up – one moment I was watching him, then he would dash off to a string of meetings. He would just have time to drop me off at the hostel.

Even at that stage, life with him was a life without him. He did not even pretend that I would have some special claim to his time.

So if you are looking for some kind of romance, you won't find it. What he always did was to see to it that one comrade was there to pick me up. Even if I didn't see him for a week, I would be industriously collected and taken back to the hostel every day, and then of course the car must dash back to fetch him and take him to his meetings. I never had any frivolous romance with him – there never was time for that.

He took me to meet a lot of his friends. Almost every night there were consultations in the suburbs; there were meetings in the townships. Nobody asked questions, people were just comrades. I was also extremely involved in my own way, in my social work, in a lot of cultural activities and a large number of women's organizations.

One day, Nelson just pulled up on the side of the road and said, 'You know, there is a woman, a dressmaker, you must go and see her, she is going to make your wedding-gown. How many bridesmaids would you like to have?' That's how I was told I was getting married to him! It was not put arrogantly; it was just something that was taken for granted. I asked, 'What time?' I was madly in love with him at that stage, and so was he with me in his own way. It was such a mutual feeling and understanding that we didn't have to talk about it.

He arranged for me to be driven to Pondoland to tell my family. I got there and for a whole day I couldn't bring myself to speak of it to my father. And then I couldn't do it directly, I told him through my stepmother. He was very shocked. Nelson was held in such high esteem and was such an important person in the country that my father couldn't imagine how I had found my way to him when I had been sent to do social work. My father was extremely proud.

But the family were also very concerned about the fact that Nelson had three children* and that I might not be able to cope. I never knew when he actually got divorced: I couldn't bring myself to ask such a thing right through our so-called courtship. And they were concerned about Nelson's future – after all, he was on trial for treason. Well, they were able to read history better than I was. But one become so much part and parcel of Nelson if you knew him that you automatically expected anything that happened to him to happen to yourself, and it didn't really matter. He gave you such confidence, such faith and courage. If you became involved in our cause as he was, it was just not possible to think in terms of yourself at all.

For him it was a total commitment which goes back to the days of his youth. Growing up in that tribal set-up in the countryside seemed to give him his background; he is a traditionalist. I don't mean in the stifled, narrow sort of way. Rather in the sense that what he is in the struggle, he is because of the love of his country, the love of his roots. He used to philosophize about the elders – white-haired, heavily bearded old men smoking their pipes beside the huge fireplaces outside the *kraal* – about their wisdom which he admired so much. It was those elders who instilled that pride in him, and love of his people. It's an incredibly strong bond – he himself as a person comes second to this love for his people, and the love of nature.

In June 1958 he was granted four days' permission to leave Johannesburg for us to get married – besides being an accused in the Treason Trial he was also banned – and I insisted on getting married at home in Pondoland, because nothing could have pleased my father better and I wanted Nelson to see my background. It was an initiation for the kind of life we were heading for anyway because we had to dash back without even completing the usual marriage ceremony in the traditional manner. After the marriage in my home, we were supposed to then get married in his home as well. As far as the elders in the family are concerned, we haven't finished getting married to this day.

It was both a traditional marriage and to some extent a Western

---

*Nelson's two sons and his daughter lived with their mother in Johannesburg.

ceremony. Of course Nelson paid *lobola** for me; I never found out how much it was. It is not talked of in terms of money but in terms of cattle. (For years, Brigadier Coetzee, who is now head of the Security Branch, kept Nelson's letter from my father, in which he acknowledged the *lobola*. And during my interrogation in 1969, I remember this horrible Swanepoel saying: 'Poor Nelson, he must have been terribly stranded to pay so much for a woman like you!')

The day Nelson comes out of prison, we must go and complete the second part of our ceremony. I still have the wedding cake, the part of that cake we were supposed to have taken to his place. I brought it here to Brandfort. It crumbled a bit when they dumped our things. It is now in my house in Orlando, waiting for him.

REMINISCENCES OF ADELAIDE JOSEPH

Among the Mandelas' close friends were Adelaide and Paul Joseph. Adelaide worked with Winnie in the Women's Federation and Paul, a senior member of the Indian Congress, was with Mandela in the Defiance Campaign and was among the defendants in the Treason Trial. Adelaide recalls those years:

I remember going with Winnie to classes where women were learning how to make public speeches. Winnie and I didn't know how to speak, so we used to write out speeches and would speak to a group of women and then they would criticize us. This is how we started learning. And when she made her first public speech – it was after she joined the Women's Federation – right on the spot, while she was speaking, the women composed a song for Winnie Mandela. And they started to sing right in the hall.

We had a handicapped child who needed a lot of treatment and medicines are so expensive in South Africa. Winnie would make sure that she got the medicines for me from the hospitals. And she gave me tremendous support in taking care of that child. And she and Nelson would drive from one institution to the other to find a place for our boy.

*A symbol of 'bride price'.

Nelson was busy twenty-four hours a day. But when he came from one of his late meetings, he would often pop in in the middle of the night when he saw our lights burning, just to check if everything was OK.

Also the sentimental side of it: he was in prison and he called me, and when I visited him, he said, 'It's Winnie's birthday and I want you to go and buy her a present.' And I remember, I bought her a dress and she was so thrilled because Nelson had remembered.

The impression of the Mandela family in the township was unbelievable. One Sunday Nelson took us around in the car. What an experience! He wanted to show us Orlando while Winnie was at home preparing lunch. Every road and street we turned into, people were shouting 'Mandela, Mandela'. They knew that car and they knew that man. That was in 1960. There wasn't a woman or child that spotted him, that didn't signal, greet him and shout his name. Then I realized that this was the man South Africa needed. There was no doubt about that. But no matter how high his position had become politically, he never forgot the people down at the bottom.

Neither did she. In her capacity as a social worker she visited the families whose husbands or sons or wives were in prison to get comprehensive case histories and sent them out to Europe so that aid could be sent to these families. She said, these are not the Mandelas, but the Dlaminis or whatever their name was, the forgotten people.

When Paul was in prison, Winnie and I used to take turns in bringing him food. So she took food to him one day and when I went there the next day they said, 'Who was that black woman? Is that your servant that you send to bring food for your husband?' I just refused to answer them. The next time Winnie brought food, they started abusing and assaulting her. She didn't say who she was. They actually broke her arm. And then she said, 'Can I see the station commander, I want to lay charges.' When the station commander came, he got the shock of his life, because he saw that it was Winnie. There was nothing he could do but to accept Winnie's charges.

EXTRACT FROM A LETTER FROM NELSON
MANDELA ON ROBBEN ISLAND TO HELEN JOSEPH*

Helen Joseph and Lilian Ngoyi were the only women defendants throughout the four and a half years of the Treason Trial. She and Mandela often drove together to Pretoria, where the trial took place in a court which had once been a synagogue.

15.10.78

Our dearest Helen,

Yes, I got your terrific letter. How you can inspire others! Your congratulations and good wishes had a tremendous effect on me. They wrenched me off this island, out of my cell and put me right in the centre of the Golden City, in Soweto, in Gould and Pritchard, on the road to Pretoria and back, and into the lovely cottage at 35 Fanny Avenue.

My mind carries a picture that never fades in spite of the years that have passed since I last saw you. You were standing in front of the house, like one waiting for the chickens to come home to roost. Zami [i.e. Winnie] and Co were outside the gate talking lively to one another. There has always been something of the British Isles in that home, serving as a crossroad in a vast sea. Few were surprised to see them there. At that time I was travelling, worried that I had left behind Zami all alone. Strange as that may sound in the circumstances, the fact that you were still there comforted me. I was confident that you would always play the role of guardian angel to her ... Perhaps that is one of the reasons why the picture is unforgettable. But not even in my wildest dream did I ever suspect that I would again hear from you. Least of all, that I would have the opportunity of including your picture in the family album. Of course, Zami and the children often speak of you, especially after May last year. In her June letter she mentioned Zazi's [granddaughter]

*British-born Helen Joseph was originally a social worker in South Africa. A founding member of the multiracial Federation of African Women, she was one of the organizers of the Congress of the People in Kliptown in 1955, where delegates of all races adopted the Freedom Charter (see pp. 151–6), the blueprint of the future South African society, and she played a key role in organizing the women's great protests against the Pass Laws in 1956. She was the first person to be placed under house arrest. Her friendship with the Mandela family dates back to the fifties. Helen Joseph is now in her eighties and remains an active opponent of apartheid.

christening ceremony and your special flight to Bloemfontein for the great occasion. She left the fuller description to Zindzi who tenderly referred to you in some detail. But the real surprise was yours which came two weeks later, followed by several photos from Muzi.*

I immediately spotted a tall lady who stood upright like a field marshal. From her defiant and graceful pose, she seemed to enjoy carrying her seventy-three years. I got the snaps on 30 July and you will be interested to know that they have reached my cell the other day. Old friends in my Section have not forgotten her and were just as keen to keep them. But now they are back in the cell and make me feel that I also witnessed the christening ceremony. It is fitting that you should be godmother to Zazi and for Dr Moroka to be godfather ... that is a tremendous combination. I sincerely hope that when Zazi grows up, that combination will be one of the driving forces in her life. No wonder Zami was so 'radiant and beautiful'.

I am sorry that Zindzi has to live so far from you. My wish has always been that she should be near you, so that you can help Zami in guiding her. This is especially the case at her present age and with her ambitions. She and Zeni [elder daughter] were too young when we parted and Zami's kind of life has brought a lot of emotional suffering on them. I always encourage them to come over to you whenever they can. It must have been a terrible blow to you to lose the old cat. I know how you loved it and how it was attached to you. I hope Lolita is equally attached and gives you the same pleasure as the old one. German shepherds are considered intelligent and reliable animals. I trust that Kwacha represents her breed well. That you have some company in the house is a source of comfort to me.

Cape Town cannot supply me with a photo album of at least 24 x 30cm to hold one of Zami's portraits. Please check whether that size is available there. But on no account should you buy one because it will not be given to me. I have enough funds to order it from this end. Finally, Helen, I should like to take this opportunity to thank you and all those who look after Zami and the children in my absence. The heat of the summer and the winter colds would have been difficult to bear without you all. I am keeping my right hand clean and warm because it has an important duty to perform, i.e. to hold yours very firmly. Meantime, your message of congratulations and good wishes has cut down my age by half. Perhaps, if I had received

*Prince Thumbumuzi Dlamini, husband of Zeni, elder daughter of Winnie and Nelson Mandela.

from JHB more than your message and that of Ismail Ayob, I would
feel even younger ... Never mind, I feel and move like a lightweight
in spite of the 76kg I carry.

SHARPEVILLE AND THE TREASON TRIAL:
MANDELA LEADS THE STRUGGLE

Our life as a family continued to be just as abnormal. Each morning
Nelson would go to the Treason Trial in Pretoria and I was out in
Orlando. Most of the time he put up in Pretoria where they prepared
the defence with this large team of lawyers. And when he did come
home, he often had executive meetings with the ANC. He pitched up
just in time to jump into the bath, change his clothes and dash for his
transport to the Treason Trial. He never had time even to eat. I had to
force him. He would sit down and begin to eat, the phone would ring:
he had to go and bail somebody at some police station. Whilst he was
away, I received a string a people whose friends and relatives had been
detained who wanted him to bail them out.

So there never was any kind of life that I can recall as family life, a
young bride's life, where you sit with your husband and dream dreams
of what life might have been, even if we knew that it would never be
like that.

You just couldn't tear Nelson from the people, from the struggle.
The nation came first. Everything else was second. His commitment is
total, yet he exudes this love. The love we have known from him, my
children and I, I don't think we would ever find anywhere else. The
understanding, the faith, the confidence he gives us – even when it is
shared by the whole nation, he always makes you feel, at the same time,
that you are special to him. I knew when I married him that I married
the struggle, the liberation of my people. But the little time we had
together, he was very affectionate.

He never had time even to know to what extent I was committed and
I couldn't get myself to ask him if I should join the other women in
their anti-pass demonstration, because I knew of our problem: he was
no longer working, and in my job, what I was earning was just enough
for food. I knew I would lose the job if I demonstrated. But I did join
in the protest against the issue of passes to women – that was in 1958.

And when he got home, he didn't find me there, I had been arrested. The Treason Trial dragged on. I was working at Baragwanath Hospital – I had been the first black medical social worker in the country – but after I was arrested, I lost my job.

I was politically influenced by his friends I spent more time with – by tremendous women like the late Lilian Ngoyi,* whom I greatly admired. She made me in the sense that I idolized her. There were little ideological differences, but the women who were close to Nelson, whom I was with daily, taught me a great deal. They were just a continuation of Nelson. In the leadership of the Federation of South African Women were Albertina Sisulu, Florence Matomela, Frances Baard, Kate Molale and Ruth Mompati, my husband's secretary, who also played a prominent role in my political outlook. These were people at the top of the ANC hierarchy. I admired them very much and I learned from them what the struggle was all about.

And of course Helen Joseph, whom I have regarded completely as my mother, because of what she has meant to me not only politically, but from a completely human point of view. There were great women like Hilda Bernstein,† Ruth First;‡ there was the Naidoo family.§ When I was with them, I felt I was with Nelson.

I held the same positions in the Federation of South African Women as I had in the ANC Women's League: I was chairlady of our branch and I belonged to the provincial executive and national executive. That was really the scope and banner under which women could operate legally in this country.

In 1958 we had been involved in organizing the anti-pass demon-

*One of the most important and powerful black women leaders; President of the Women's League of the ANC and later of the Federation of South African Women, she organized the resistance campaigns of the women from 1952; one of the accused in the Treason Trial of 1956–61; banned for eleven years.

†Hilda Bernstein, active in the Women's Federation, had spent three years during the 1940s on the Johannesburg City Council as its only communist member. Her husband, Lionel, was among the defendants in the Rivonia Trial.

‡Ruth First, Johannesburg editor of radical newspapers, author of several books on African topics, co-author of a biography of Olive Schreiner, and an academic. She and her husband, advocate Joe Slovo, were at the heart of the liberation struggle. In August 1982, while she was heading an international team of academics investigating the lives of migrant labourers in Mozambique, she was killed by a letter bomb.

§The Naidoo family has played a leading role in the Indian Congress since Gandhi's early years in South Africa.

strations under the leadership of Lilian Ngoyi. I was among thousands of women arrested throughout the country. I was pregnant at the time, and Albertina Sisulu saved my first baby. She went out of her way in prison to look after me.

The Women's Federation was never banned. All they did was to ban every member of the executive in an attempt to destroy the organization. I was also involved in cultural activities and the Margaret Ballinger home for blind and deaf children. These were sidelines of my political activities.

But with more and more restrictions it became impossible for me to function in any sphere of life.

In those early years of our marriage, my husband used to embarrass me – he had a strange sense of humour, he almost drove me to tears. When his friends jocularly asked, where on earth he'd met this little girl, and why her – they were so frank when we went to these ANC parties where he rarely pitched up since he never had time; he would come at the end to pick me up – he would joke and say he was my political saviour, that he had salvaged me from the Conventionists. And then, one of his terrible jokes was about my work – I was dealing with broken bones and accident cases and he said I had promised to get him all the WCA cases – WCA means Workman Compensation Act – because he was such a good attorney, in return for marriage! He pulls those jokes with a very straight face – you have to know him to understand.

One of the stories he used to tell was how he was coming from court when he saw an old lady whose car had broken down in the middle of Commissioner Street, an old white lady. So he helped the lady push the car. And when it started again, she took 5c from her pocket. So he thanks her, saying, 'No, no, never mind, thank you very much.' She jumped out of her car, stood with her hands on her hips and said, 'Look at this Kaffir! He wants 25c! Well, you won't get it from me!' He loved to tell these stories.

Another day when he was walking down Commissioner Street, a black man was standing at the door of a shop – calling customers to come inside. And there was an old Jewish chap inside, the owner. The black man literally drags Nelson into the shop – obviously he was paid commission. So Nelson obliges and walks in. The white man tries to sell him a pair of trousers, this black man tries to sell him a hat, a stetson, bottle green, shouting green, then the white man comes along and tries to sell him another hat. So Nelson calmly takes the stetson – he never wore hats – just because it was a black man who had to get a plate of food by selling him something. Of course he never wore it. That is why we never had a cent to our name. So he came home, dangling this hat – we threw it away. Brand new, it was so expensive! He paid for it because a black man had been pleading with him to buy it. That's typical – he was an economic disaster at home. He never had a cent in his pocket. If he went and defended two or three cases that day and happened to have R10 in his pocket, he would take his little daughter Zeni and buy her pretty dresses – she was only about two years old – and then he would buy boxes and boxes of fruit; he was a health fanatic – it had to be high-protein food and vegetables! And of course he was training every day! And that's what happened to the little funds we had.

We always lived in cramped conditions. Incidentally, he chose the little shack in Orlando himself. He was working for the Johannesburg City Council, when they were building up Orlando – it was in the 1940s. And one day the Superintendent, who was his boss at the time, told Mandela to go and choose a house. So he went and chose the smallest; typical of him! He chose a corner house which was just a kitchen, a bedroom and a front room – that's all. And he was the first resident there. He could have chosen the one next door which was four rooms! He is like that. He must have the last in everything in life.

There has never been a stage in my life where it was my husband and I and the children. He would come home from court and say, 'Darling, I brought my friends here to taste your lovely cooking,' and he would pitch up with ten people and we would have one chop in the fridge.

I used to be reduced to tears and he would laugh and run around looking for a packet of tinned fish from the local shops. He is just like that. He never had a banking account. He couldn't possibly have one.

We became such total colleagues and comrades in the struggle that there was no such thing as him reporting to me when he was going to his meetings. I just took it for granted, when he was going to whole-night sessions of the executive meetings and would come home and not find me, he would know that I had gone to my own meetings. We never even asked, how was it, at the end of the day. It was part of the life of that house.

1960 was proclaimed Africa Year at the United Nations, celebrating international acceptance of the principle of African independence after the long history of colonialism. Chief Lutuli, President-General of the ANC, called for an international boycott of South African goods.

In South Africa it was the year of Sharpeville, when police fired at a crowd of peacefully gathered men, women and children protesting against the Pass Laws. 69 were killed and 176 wounded. As outrage swept the world, massive demonstrations shook South Africa. The government declared a State of Emergency: police and army rounded up some 2,000 leaders and organizers as well as many thousands of 'vagrants'. The ANC was outlawed, as was the break-away Pan Africanist Congress, which under the leadership of Robert Sobukwe had called the original protest against the Pass Laws. The ANC's last legal act was to call for a National Convention to lay the foundation for a new Union of all South Africans – a call which, twenty years later, was to be taken up by leaders of the Parliamentary opposition.

The UN Security Council, by nine votes to none, with Britain and France abstaining, condemned the South African government for the shootings and called on it to initiate measures to bring about racial harmony based on equality.

Mandela and the other 29 defendants who had been out on bail through the long years of the Treason Trial, were among those held in Pretoria prison. The defence team, which included several of South Africa's most distinguished advocates, withdrew, protesting that it was impossible to function in a political trial during a state of emergency. During their absence, Mandela and Duma Nokwe, an advocate, took over the defence and, in jail, prepared the other accused for the continuing case. Mandela also gave evidence. In the course of the State's cross-examination, he was asked by the Judge whether African freedom was not a direct threat to the Europeans.

'We are not anti-white,' he replied, 'we are against white supremacy and, in struggling against white supremacy, we have the support of some sections of the European population ... It is quite clear that the ANC has consistently preached a policy of race harmony and we have condemned racialism no matter by whom it is professed.' The Congress demanded universal adult franchise, he added, and economic pressure, defiance campaigns and stay-at-home strikes would be the weapons used, until the government was prepared to talk.

Released from prison after five months, he could return home to Winnie and their small child, Zenani. A second daughter, Zindziswa, was born in December. But when the Treason Trial, after intermittent adjournments, resumed, each day there was again the long drive to and from the court.

On 29 March 1961 the 30 defendants awaited the verdict. In 'findings of fact' the Judge said that the State had failed to prove a policy of violence and that, although a 'strong left-wing tendency' had manifested itself, the State had not proved that the ANC was communist or that the Freedom Charter pictured a communist state. 'You are found Not Guilty,' he announced. 'You may go.'

Two weeks earlier, Mandela's banning orders had expired and had not been renewed. For the first time in nine years he was free to attend gatherings and to speak freely.

South Africa was about to become a republic – a 'white Boer republic', the Africans called it. Treated as non-citizens, they, as always, had gone unconsulted. An All-In African Conference was organized in Pietermaritzburg – 1,400 delegates from all parts of the country attended. Unexpectedly, Mandela appeared to deliver the main speech. The effect was electrifying. He was elected to organize protests against the white republic, and to demand a National Convention. Should the government not respond, he was to call for a general strike.

The government ordered a fresh round of arrests.

I Always Waited for
That Sacred Knock

LIFE UNDERGROUND

'It was the most inspiring time of his life – he was totally with them, totally part of the people he has sacrificed his life for. He lived among them. And to see him with his people was one of the most inspiring things, even to me.'

At the end of the Treason Trial in 1961, Nelson came home with Duma Nokwe and other leaders of the outlawed ANC, and he simply said, 'Oh, darling, just pack a few things for me in a suitcase.' He was outside the gate, but I couldn't reach him there were so many people wishing him well – everybody was excited. I packed his bag, but by the time I took it out, he wasn't there. He was gone. Someone else came to fetch the bag about an hour later.

In the afternoon papers on the following day I read that he had emerged in Pietermaritzburg and addressed a convention I knew nothing about. I had not even realized that his banning order had expired at that time.

That was the last I saw of my husband as a family man, legally at home. There had been no chance to sit down and discuss his decision to commit himself totally.

I think he found it too hard to tell me. With all that power and strength he exudes, he is so soft inside. I had just noticed that week that he was silent and thoughtful, and I remember asking whether anything was worrying him. And then, before washing his shirt one day, I found a document in the pocket. He had paid rent for six months – that was very unusual. So I think he was trying to ease the pain, trying to think of ways in which I would be able to face life more easily without him. And then the car. It was not in order, and he suddenly had it repaired, and just left it parked in the garage.

That was the day he went underground. Then followed extremely difficult days.

I had so little time to love him, and that love has survived all these years of separation. I'm not trying to suggest that he is an angel. Perhaps if I'd had time to know him better I might have found a hell of a lot of faults, but I only had time to love him and to long for him all the time.

I saw him frequently when he was underground. We had a very dramatic life. I waited for that sacred knock at the window in the early hours of the morning. I never knew when. I never had an appointment made. At the beginning he used to come home for an hour or so early in the morning, depending on the political situation. Later, they were watching me twenty-four hours a day and I had to slip out through police cordons to go to him.

Then, someone would come and order me to follow him in my car. We would drive a kilometre or so from the house, we would then meet another car, we would jump from that one into another, and by the time I reached him I had gone through something like ten cars. I never knew where I was. His hideouts were all over the country.

The people who arranged this were, of course, mostly whites. I don't know to this day who they were. I would just find myself at the end of the journey in some white house; in most cases when we got there they were deserted. You could see that arrangements had been made for families to stay away while we were there together.

MEETING UNDERGROUND

Sally Motlana, an old friend of the family who has been involved in various political organizations for many years, remembers an evening during that time:

'I had received a telephone call that a visitor would be coming. The door bell rang at 8 p.m. I almost dropped dead when I saw *him* standing outside.

'"Do me a favour and fetch Winnie," he said. And I rushed off to get her. "Make yourself as beautiful as you can," I told her, "an important personality wants to see you." We drove back and I took her to a room at the far end of the house. "Do you want to kill me," she asked jokingly? Then I only heard the happy laughter of the two. We left them alone and dropped Nelson in town around midnight.'

Mandela, a well-known public figure on whom the police had a large dossier, and a tall, striking man, could not easily go unrecognized; as he contrived to travel the country organizing the forthcoming protest strike against the new republic, not only he, but all those he contacted, had to get used to wholly new methods.

In an open letter to the Press he explained that going underground was the only course left open despite the hardship it entailed: 'I have had to separate myself from my dear wife and children, from my mother and sisters, to live as an outlaw in my own land. I have had to abandon my profession and live in poverty, as many of my people are doing ... The struggle,' he concluded, 'is my life.'

In making the demand for a National Convention, he not only wrote to the Prime Minister but to the Leader of the Parliamentary Opposition, calling for support – an appeal which went unanswered. To Dr Verwoerd he deplored the 'savage attacks on the rights and living conditions of the African people' under a government 'notorious the world over for its obnoxious policies'. The dangerous situation could only be averted by the calling of a convention 'to draw up a non-racial and democratic constitution'. Unless that happened before Republic Day on 31 May 1961, there would be a country-wide stay-at-home of black workers on the 29th. Mandela added, 'We are not deterred by threats of force and violence.'

Wide-ranging arrests followed; there was a massive call-up of police and army; townships were raided; employers threatened to sack all strikers: yet on 29 May, in Johannesburg and Pretoria more than 60 per cent of African labour responded to the strike call, and in Port Elizabeth 75 per cent. Next day, in secret meetings with journalists, Mandela was asked if he conceded that the strike had been a failure. 'In the light of the steps taken by the government to suppress it, it was a tremendous success,' he replied, pointing out what courage it had taken all those hundreds of thousands of men and women to defy police and army. 'If the government reaction is to crush by naked force our non-violent struggle, we will have to seriously reconsider

*our tactics,' he added. 'In my mind, we are closing a chapter on this question
of a non-violent policy.'*

*Mandela remained underground, at times staying at a farm in Rivonia,
an outlying suburb of Johannesburg.*

At Lilliesleaf in Rivonia I was able for the first time to cook meals
for Nelson and the children and retain something of a family life. It was
then the headquarters of the organization. And the whole farm was so
divided, that in this portion we could – at least for the few hours I was
there – live like a real family. Nelson would take the children for walks
in the rambling garden. So Zeni imagined that to be her home, because
it was the only place where her father had played with her. For years
after, she dreamt of this home and asked me, 'Mummy, when are we
going home to see Daddy?'

Her marriage to Muzi and the environment where they live in
Swaziland I think reminds her of those days. And with the first few
wages they got, they found themselves a farmhouse which is something
like Lilliesleaf. It has never left her mind that that was her home.

And of course the narrow shaves we had there with the police – my
robustness helped me so many times, because we invariably ran into
road blocks. Once I feigned labour pains. I was huge, my face has
always been round and I did look pregnant all the time. So the first time
we ran into this road block – I was with a doctor, fortunately, who was
driving a car with a Red Cross sign – the only logical thing to do was
just to lie back and feign labour pains. I was gasping and sweating and
they let us through.

I remember another occasion when the crock of a car Nelson left me
with gave in completely. Someone came to me at work that day and
told me to drive to a particular corner. When I got there, a tall man in
blue overalls and a chauffeur's white coat and peaked cap opened the
door, ordered me to shift from the driver's seat and took over and drove.
That was him. He had a lot of disguises and he looked so different that
for a moment, when he walked towards the car, I didn't recognize him
myself. In broad daylight he drove to a garage and bought me a car,
trading in the old crock, then drove me to the centre of Johannesburg.
And in the thick of Sauer Street, where there are hundreds of com-
muters, he just stopped at a 'Stop' sign, got out, bade me goodbye and
disappeared. So that was the kind of life we led.

While he was touring Africa and visiting London, we kept in touch by correspondence. I never knew how he sent the letters through.

And he had journeyed all over South Africa. It was the most inspiring time of his life – he was totally with them, totally part of the people he has sacrificed his life for. He lived among them. And to see him with his people was one of the most inspiring things, even to me.

In December 1961, six months after Mandela had spoken of 'closing a chapter' on the question of a non-violent policy, sabotage against government installations marked the emergence of Umkhonto we Sizwe – 'Spear of the Nation'. As he later explained, Umkhonto (MK) was a reaction to the violence of the system: 'The Nationalist government has rejected every peaceable demand by the people for rights and freedom, and answered every such demand with force and yet more force. The time comes in the life of any nation when there remains only two choices: submit or fight.' (The Preamble to the Universal Declaration of Human Rights is relevant: 'It is essential if man is not to be compelled to have recourse, as a last resort, to rebellion against tyranny and oppression, that human rights should be protected by the Rule of Law.')

International recognition of the ANC's long record – over half a century – of non-violent action, came almost simultaneously with the award to Chief Albert Lutuli of the Nobel Peace Prize.

Mandela, already South Africa's most hunted man, continued to elude the police, and early in 1962 slipped out of the country to address a Pan-African conference in Addis Ababa before visiting heads of state in a number of African countries. He then went to London, where he met the leaders of the Labour and Liberal parties, and to Algeria for a course of military training.

For the first time in his life, he was to say, he had felt a free man: 'Free from white oppression, from the idiocy of apartheid and racial arrogance, from police molestation, from humiliation and indignity. Wherever I went I was treated like a human being. In the African states I saw black and white mingling peacefully and happily in hotels, cinemas; trading in the same areas, using the same public transport, and living in the same residential areas.'

Secretly he returned to South Africa. During his absence sabotage had continued. In Johannesburg he reported on his tour to the National High Command of Umkhonto, and then set off for Natal to report to the regional command. Returning from there, on 5 August 1962, he was captured, apparently on a tip-off from an informer.

I saw Nelson only once when he returned from abroad, a hurried meeting – our last private moments together.

The way I got the news of his arrest was terrible. I was at work at the Child Welfare offices and I was on my way out, going to do field-work in the Soweto area. I went down in the lift and, as I was getting out, I bumped into one of his friends – the way this man looked! He was white like a ghost, his hair was standing on end. I noticed he hadn't shaved and was wearing a dirty shirt and trousers as if he'd just jumped out of bed; you could see something drastic had happened. This was one of the men who used to be along the line when I was taken to see Nelson underground.

I associated him so much with my husband that I found myself asking, 'Is he all right?' The first thing that struck me was that Nelson had been injured. And I thought, my God, he could have run into a road block and the police could have fired. And the reply was, 'No, we think he'll be appearing in the Johannesburg court tomorrow.' Then of course I knew what that meant.

It was the collapse of a political dream. At that moment I wasn't only shocked for myself. I was shocked for the struggle and what it meant for the cause of my people – then, when he was at the height of his political career.

I don't know how I reached home. I just remember, vaguely, throwing my files in the back of my car and driving straight home. Fortunately my sister was there to console me. Of course I have since recovered from the painful shock. I knew at that time that this was the end of any kind of family life, as was the case with millions of my people – I was no exception.

Part of my soul went with him at that time.

Mandela was put on trial, charged with inciting Africans to strike in May 1961, and with leaving the country without valid travel documents. Conducting his own defence, he used the dock as a place from which to challenge the government and the white electorate with the history and realities of the life of his people and their long struggle. 'The government,' he said, 'set out not to treat with us, not to heed us, not to talk to us, but rather to present us as wild, dangerous revolutionaries, intent on disorder and riot, incapable of being dealt with in any way save by mustering an overwhelming force against us and the implementation of every forcible means, legal and illegal, to suppress us.' Sentenced to five years with hard labour, he avowed that when he was released he would still be moved 'to take up the struggle for the removal of injustices until they are finally abolished once and for all'.

Winnie Mandela was present in court, with his aunt and other relatives from the Transkei. Afterwards she said, 'I will continue the fight as I have in all ways done in the past.'

THE RIVONIA TRIAL

Meanwhile, throughout the country, sabotage against Bantu Administration offices and other symbols of apartheid continued. Umkhonto's hoped-for impact on the economy – the deterring of foreign investors – was unfulfilled, but State retaliation revealed deep fear. A new Minister of Justice, B. J. Vorster, passed the 'ninety-day law', giving Security Police the right to detain people without charge, in solitary confinement, incommunicado, for successive periods of 90 days, while interrogating them until their answers were 'satisfactory'. Thousands were arrested. Soon came evidence of police torture and the first death of a detainee undergoing interrogation.

On 12 July 1963 the police made their most spectacular coup, capturing Walter Sisulu and six other men at Lilliesleaf farm. When the Rivonia Trial opened in Pretoria on 9 October 1963 the Palace of Justice was surrounded by armed police. The defendants included Dennis Goldberg and other Umkhonto organizers, as well as Ahmed Kathrada, an Indian Congress activist since his schooldays, and ANC leaders such as Sisulu and Govan Mbeki from the Eastern Cape.

Nelson Mandela was Accused No. 1. Called on to plead, he led the others in stating: 'The government should be in the dock, not me. I plead not guilty.'

The State case depended largely on a mass of documents captured at Lilliesleaf and on the evidence of turncoats, much of which was discredited. Defence counsel warned the accused that they were likely to be charged with attempting to overthrow the government and that the penalty, if they were found guilty, was death. The defendants made it clear they were not interested in a trial in law, but in a political confrontation. They readily admitted that several of them had taken part in a campaign of sabotage designed to bring down the government and that provision was made for the eventual possibility of guerrilla warfare. They wholly repudiated charges of conspiring to bring about a foreign invasion.

The United Nations reflected worldwide anger with an unprecedented, unanimous vote of 106, calling for the immediate release of the Rivonia men and of all South Africa's political prisoners.

On Monday 23 April 1964 the court was packed. Winnie Mandela accompanied her mother-in-law who had arrived from the Transkei. Bram Fischer, QC, leading counsel, announced that the defence case would commence with a statement from the dock by Nelson Mandela, 'who personally took part in the establishment of Umkhonto and who will be able to inform the court of the beginnings of that organization'.

Mandela opened his statement: 'At the outset, I want to say that the suggestion made by the State that the struggle in South Africa is under the influence of foreigners or communists is wholly incorrect. I have done whatever I did, both as an individual and as a leader of my people, because of my experience in South Africa and my own proudly felt African background, and not because of what any outsider might have said.'

Umkhonto had been founded, he said, because 'we believed that as a result of government policy, violence by the African people had become inevitable, and that unless responsible leadership was given to canalize and control the feelings of our people, there would be outbreaks of terrorism which would produce an intensity of bitterness and hostility between the various races of this country which is not produced even by war'. The form of action they had chosen, sabotage, 'did not involve loss of life, and offered the best hope for future race relations', and strict instructions had been given to Umkhonto members on no account to injure or kill people – instructions which had been confirmed by State witnesses.

As for the State allegation that the aims of the ANC and the Communist Party were the same, he said that the creed of the ANC had always been African nationalism, but that there was close cooperation with the CP: they had a common goal, the removal of white supremacy. For many decades communists had been the only political group prepared to treat Africans as human beings and equals, the only group prepared to work with Africans in their struggle to attain political rights and a stake in society. 'And in the *international field,' he added, 'communist countries have always come to our aid ... [and] often seem more sympathetic to our plight than some of the Western powers.' He gave a graphic statement of what Africans wanted, and concluded:*

> Above all, we want equal political rights, because without them our disabilities will be permanent. I know this sounds revolutionary to the whites in the country, because the majority of voters will be Africans. This makes the white man fear democracy. But this fear cannot be allowed to stand in the way of the only solution which will guarantee racial harmony and freedom for all. It is not true that the enfranchisement of all will result in racial domination. Political division based on colour is entirely artificial and when it disappears, so will the domination of one colour group by another. The ANC has spent half a century fighting against racialism. When it triumphs it will not change that policy.

Albertina Sisulu, present in court, has described the atmosphere at that moment: 'It was so quiet, you could hear a pin drop. And then came the end.' Mandela looked up at the Judge and said quietly: 'During my lifetime I have dedicated myself to this struggle of the African people. I have fought against white domination, and I have fought against black domination. I have cherished the ideal of a democratic and free society in which all persons live together in harmony and with equal opportunities. It is an ideal which I hope to live for and to achieve. But if needs be, it is an ideal for which I am prepared to die.'

With that last sentence, Mrs Sisulu said, it became dark. 'To us, his people, Mandela is everything.'

In June 1964 the Judge gave his verdict: 'Nelson Mandela is found guilty ...' So it went for seven of the defendants. The eighth, Lionel Bernstein, was acquitted.

On Friday 12 June the judge announced sentence: for all the accused, 'life imprisonment'.

'I fully expected to see a shaken Mrs Mandela emerge from the courthouse,' remarked a journalist who was present. 'But no. She appeared on the steps and she flashed a smile that dazzled. The effect was regal and almost triumphant, performed in the heart of the Afrikaner capital in her moment of anguish, and the crowds of Africans thronging Church Square, with Paul Kruger's statue in the middle, loved it. They cheered, perhaps

the only time black people have ever summoned the courage to cheer in that place.'

'*To most of the world,*' *the* New York Times *commented,* '*[the Rivonia men] are heroes and freedom fighters, the George Washingtons and Ben Franklins of South Africa.*' *While* The Times *of London said,* '*The picture that emerges is of men goaded beyond endurance . . . The verdict of history will be that the ultimate guilty party is the government in power – and that already is the verdict of world opinion.*'

*Allister Sparks, *Observer*, 20 March 1983.

He Was a Pillar of Strength to Me

BEING ALONE

'We waited outside the court where they would be driven to Pretoria Central Prison, to wave goodbye to them for the last time. We were in the midst of this huge crowd – I held Zeni's hand and Zindzi was on my arm – when someone grasped my shoulder. I turned and what do I see? A huge policeman and he says: "Remember your permit! You must be back in Johannesburg by twelve o'clock."'

The last day of the Rivonia trial, the spirit was absolutely extraordinary. The atmosphere in court was extremely militant, although of course there were tears all over, but a militant type of tears, not tears of despair. There were freedom songs and slogans: 'We stand by our leaders', 'Away with racialism'.

I remember Alan Paton speaking in mitigation of sentence. He was so sincere, a real political colleague; I'll never forget him for that.

We expected the men to be sentenced for life – we knew the laws. They couldn't have taken the political risk of hanging the leadership – spirits were so high and the international pressure was at its best – the country would have been on fire.

But of course it brought about a sense of desperation. We knew our leaders would be gone, and how difficult it would be to regroup and reorganize resistance. When a struggle goes underground, it means a new pattern for your own life and a new concept for the political outlook and thinking of the people.

It is far more difficult to conscientize them under those conditions. We knew we would be heading for grim times.

81

That last day of the trial was an expression of the black man's determination to attain his freedom.

One of the most unforgettable things was the rendering of the freedom songs and the national anthem – 'Nkosi Sikelel' i-Afrika' – as a send-off for our leaders. Throughout the years they have confirmed that that type of send-off meant so much to them. When you go into detention, you have to get your inspiration from the memory of what you left behind and their spirits have remained manifest in the spirit of that day. That day we knew – whatever we were faced with – we would attain our freedom. And that this was just one of the temporary phases we had to go through. But one had to admit it was a terrible setback to our struggle. We went there resigned, we knew that we would come back without our husbands and brothers.

Mandela's speech had been a summary of the four hundred years of our suffering and a grim prophecy of what we had to expect, of the inevitable bloodshed we later witnessed in 1976; a grim prophecy of the reality of our situation thereafter, and of the possibility of us falling back in our struggle to a situation where people would resort to acts of violence and sabotage without the guidance of our leadership – precisely what they had been trying to prevent. And that was what happened. So that day was a solemn day, more of a church day than anything else. It was a great solemn send-off.

Zindzi was four and Zeni five years old. I was holding them, it was after their father and the other men had been found guilty. We waited outside where they would be driven to Pretoria Central Prison, to wave goodbye to them for the last time. There were thousands of people, it was not possible for the relatives to get close to the accused. People tried to push us in front to be able to touch the hands of the accused for a last time – it was hopeless. So we were in the midst of this huge crowd, I held Zeni's hand and Zindzi was on my arm, when someone grasped my shoulder. I turned and what do I see? A huge policeman, a member of the Security Branch, and he says, 'Remember your permit! You must be back in Johannesburg by twelve o'clock!' Here I was with my people, singing the national anthem, and there is this man with his hand on my shoulder repeating that I must go back to Johannesburg! All I could do was to kick him and ignore him. Can you imagine! The last day! My husband is sentenced to life and I must think in terms of permits and the time of day.

I saw him once more before he was sent to Robben Island. It was extremely painful. But he has this way about him of reassuring you and dispelling whatever fears you have. Just seeing him reconstructed those emotions that were falling apart and rebuilt me. He prepared me for the difficult life ahead. In fact, almost everything that has happened in these last twenty years, he prophesied. He told me, you will be vilified, you must expect that you will be told that you are responsible for my being in prison. You are young and life without a husband is full of all kinds of insults. I expect you to live up to my expectations. Each time I've seen him it has been a rebuilding of my inner soul.

There was an incident two days before Nelson was convicted. I was approached by some elders telling me that I was to be given something by a *sangoma* before I entered court and that I must put it into my shoe, so that certain things were not done to him in court by the white man. The emotional battle I fought inside! I was taught to respect my elders, and these were grey-haired men. But with my kind of upbringing I didn't believe in it and felt it would be worse to be deceptive. When I came to the Palace of Justice, they gave me a tiny little bottle with a brownish, oily liquid which looked as if it had some hairs in it. I could not bring myself to take it. I was not sufficiently mature to see that it would have done no harm and that it would have pleased the elders. I knew it wouldn't have any effect on Nelson, who was supposed to be released by these herbs. He would have wanted to fight for his liberation and not get it through herbs! When they were sentenced, of course, the elders said, 'There you are! You see! A young thing like this did not want him to be released from jail!' They sincerely believed this. I had sold him to the white man because I didn't want to conform to the traditions and customs of my people.

In the earlier years I was just a carbon copy of Nelson. I was no individual. If I said something, it was 'Nelson's wife' who said so. When he was no longer in the picture (I so hate talking about myself!), the public began to say, I wasn't just a carbon copy as such; I had ideas and views of my own. I had my own commitment and I wasn't just a political ornament.

Looking at our struggle in this country, the black woman has had to struggle a great deal, not only from a political angle. One has had to fight the male domination in a much more complex sense. We have the cultural clash where a black woman must emerge as a politician against the traditional background of a woman's place being at home! Of course most cultures are like that. But with us it's not only pronounced by law. We are permanent minors by law. So for a woman to emerge as an individual, as a politician in this context, is not very easy.

If you read the court records of the time, you can see the systematic slandering of my name by the government: those affairs with just about everybody with whom I had contacts.

Peter Magubane, the photographer, for instance, was not banned because he was a security risk. The idea was that he shouldn't be able to communicate with us and therefore wouldn't be able to help the children. The reason why Magubane spent so much time in prison was purely because he gave so much help to Nelson's children.

His business with me was presented as political, but the whole reason was to punish him for that in such a way that we suffered indirectly; this is what they have done to everybody who has come to our assistance. Even granny – Helen Joseph – did not have the vicious attacks on her before we became so close. They escalated and became more and more vicious as I drifted closer to her and treated her as the mother she subsequently became to me. She has suffered a great deal. She is just one example, but this has happened to everybody who was close to us.

About Peter's trials: the whole reason for trying us was that we attempted to communicate when we were not supposed to. Yet the state tried to reduce them to something a little cheaper than that. 'Finding a man in Mandela's house' – these would be the screaming headlines. We have the gutter press; they have their men in our newspapers and would use them to work on the mind of the public to present a picture of something more undignified than a political trial. This is the pattern of these people.

They used their gutter reporters in our press. One such reporter – Gumbi was his name, he was working for the *Post*, they used him for years – would write the article in such a way that it becomes so suggestive. Invariably, that type of article will find its way under the door of my husband's cell in prison. There isn't a single one of those cases he is not aware of. This is what has been happening throughout the years. Any case which was supposed to be slanderous, he would find a copy of an article under his door. At one time he indicated to me that a copy of a letter I had written to a friend years ago found its way under the cell. He expected that type of thing. There is this generation gap between us. They never expected me to live up to it. They thought that, as the years went by, they were going to break me and that I would throw in the towel and go back to my father.

The first few weeks and months after Nelson was gone, that was utter hell. Solitude, loneliness, is worse than fear – the most wretchedly painful illness the body and mind could be subjected to. When you suddenly realize that you are stripped of a man of such formidable stature, of whom you were just a shadow, you find yourself absolutely naked. He was a pillar of strength to me. I fumbled along and tried to adjust. It was extremely difficult. His lovely letters helped me most during that time. I couldn't see him for six months and he was allowed only one letter in that time. That one letter I kept re-reading until the first six months expired.

I had been looking forward to leading a married life one day and having a home; it sustains you. You keep looking forward to that love which you cannot enjoy. I think I am the most unmarried married woman. I look forward to some day – even if it will mean just a day – enjoying some kind of married life with him. I would be thankful for even that.

He misses those days at home when he would do his jogging early in the morning – he used to get up at four o'clock for his training – and I would wait with a glass of fruit juice and with some medical stuff to rub on his body after his bath. Humane things like that. It's painful to recall.

And the first thing he wants to do when he comes out of prison, is to travel to the countryside to see his people, to look at the mountains and breathe the fresh air. The love of his culture, the love of his tradition, the love of this country is so genuine and strong. He is working to liberate his people because he loves them so much – that trader from home he used to buy from as a boy in the *backveld* of the Transkei – and then there is that big bushy river that they call the Kei, where he used to sit and meditate with the elders – he misses all that most terribly. To him, liberating his country would be recapturing that dream, to see it as he visualized it as a child.

He was allowed to garden on the island – the only thing they could do in a relaxed way. Nelson once wrote me a letter about a twig. He can write a whole book just from staring at that twig. He had a few tomato plants and he inadvertently injured one of the plants he loved very much. He wrote two letters (you cannot exceed 500 words). The first letter of 500 words was not enough. He described the beauty of that tomato plant, how it grew and grew, how he was able to give it life because he nursed it, and how he inadvertently injured it and his feelings when it died. He pulled it out from the soil and washed those roots and thought of the life that might have been.

He is unable to write to me politically. Out of letters like that, you can sort of get how he feels about certain things. One could equate that with a beautifully growing child in a political situation like this, where you as a parent are able to give it whatever you can, to nurse that life, to bring it to that particular age, and then it gets mowed down by circumstances not of your making – and the feelings of the parent. One could equate this, for instance, with the mowing down of those hundreds of children in 1976. If he had written to me about that, I wouldn't have got the letter.

The one who helped me most in this difficult time was a wiry priest with a granite personality, Father Leo Rakale of the Anglican Church. He hauled me out of my shattered self. He spent hours with me at home and dragged me to hours of 'retreat' at the Rosettenville Priory, where with his aid I rediscovered the value of my soul in relation to my religious beliefs and most of all to the cause of my people.

It was this that later helped me during the seventeen months of solitary confinement in the Pretoria Central Prison. Whenever I reached rock bottom during those grim hours of depression, his ministry was a tremendous source of inspiration.

We grew so close that he became part of my family; so much so that Nelson appointed him one of the guardians of our children, the two others being my maternal uncle and Dr Nthatho Motlana.

The first visitor I received when I was charged in the Pretoria Supreme Court was Father Leo Rakale, who continued his ministry up to his death when I was in Brandfort.

My other very close friend, Father John Rushton of Bloemfontein, became an indirect replacement, together with the Dean, Father Cross, and the Bishop, Father Amoore. With these I would place one other man who was a very close friend of my husband, Ahmed Kathrada, a staunch communist according to the government, who had played a major role in inculcating in me strength, courage and determination before he was captured at Rivonia.

The difficult part was finding myself with a spotlight on me. I wasn't ready for that. I was ready to deputize for Nelson. Before, even if I battled to put my own ideas across in a meeting, it was Mandela speaking. And suddenly he was not there. And I had to think so carefully what I said – as his representative. I don't mean careful because of my banning orders but because of the responsibility.

The first time I was banned was in 1962. I had delivered one speech – the Indian Youth Congress had invited me. Years later, I asked the present head of the security branch, Johan Coetzee, about it. He is now a Major-General. He was just a young constable in those days. We have known each other that long! He was now the one I asked, what the hell they had banned me for in 1962? So he said, there is a saying in Afrikaans that if you have a field with a lot of pumpkins and you see a pig next to those pumpkins, you don't have to be told that that pig is going to eat those pumpkins.

On the strength of that type of mentality, I am serving the twentieth year of my banning orders! Because they had nothing against me at that time, except that I was Nelson's wife.

Those banning orders – during the Rivonia trial I was forbidden to leave Johannesburg. I had to get special permission to attend the court. And I was banned from wearing my traditional dress – we women all pitched up in our traditional dresses, it inspired people, it evoked militancy – but I was only allowed in court on condition that I never wore traditional dress. If I wanted to attend the trial, I had to conform. I thought, we are supposed to develop 'according to our own tradition'. But you mustn't identify with your culture *your* way, you must identify with your culture *their* way. I think I am the only black in this country who has ever been prevented from wearing her own traditional dress! So I started wearing the traditional colours of the ANC. But then I got problems too. During a court case in 1977 for instance, when I was being cross-examined, the prosecutor said, 'Mrs Mandela, can you tell this court why you have come dressed in the colours of the banned African National Congress?' I stood in the dock and said, 'Mr Prosecutor, I want to tell you that of the limited rights I still have in this country, I still have a right to choose my own wardrobe.' The prosecutor just said, 'No more questions.'

In the white courts we never plead in mitigation to any offence, no matter how petty or how much of a frame-up; this would lower the morale of the people. And in any case, you cannot plead in mitigation if you are actually innocent and those who accuse you are the real criminals.

We do well in the upper courts, but we always have to battle in the lower courts.

That's where I always feel very badly. It is difficult to win a case outright in the magistrates' or regional courts. I always expected a sentence. You seem to feel the hot air coming from the nostrils of the magistrate, breathing fumes of hostility that consume you as you are sitting there in the dock.

I don't in fact remember any junior court finding me not guilty except when I had assaulted Sergeant Fourie. The irony of it – the things I have not done, I've been found guilty of, and the only thing I did to my heart's satisfaction, I was not guilty of.

Sergeant Fourie came to my house in Orlando one day – without knocking he came in, put his hand on my shoulder and mumbled nonsense in Afrikaans which I didn't understand. I do believe it's true that people don't plan to kill. If I had had anything in my hand at that particular time, I might have killed that man. Such disrespect! Such intrusion of my privacy. I was in my bedroom, I had my skirt half-way up – heavens! – and he walked in like that, he didn't retreat and say 'excuse me'; he finds me standing in this humiliating position in the bedroom and he continues as if I'm just a piece of furniture! And then he puts his hand on my shoulder! I don't know how he landed on his neck. All I remember is grabbing him, and throwing him on the floor, which is what he deserved. I remember seeing his legs up in the air and him screaming, and the whole dressing-stand falling on him. That is how he broke his neck (he did recover). I didn't know half the army was outside. I was carried to the car by six of them – with one stocking on, one shoe; I went to prison like that!

There they said I was resisting arrest. George Bizos, our lawyer – I would listen to him as I would listen to my father. He treats me in the same way as Nelson does. He weighs the same authority with us. So he says to me outside court, 'I want you to behave like a lady in front of the magistrate and not like an Amazon!' Nelson always said to me – one of the things George and Nelson agree on – 'Zami, you are completely and utterly undisciplined! You need a great deal of taming!' I don't think I'm undisciplined. But you have to use the language they understand: to have peace, you must be violent.

I have had so many fights with the police. I don't remember, it happened all the time. And both parties have been too embarrassed to go to court.

The judges in the upper courts – one has to admit – stick to the law and listen to the reasoning of the accused.

Of course I could never appeal against my banning orders, because that's not provided for by the law.

What hurts most then, I never met a single one of my children's teachers. The very first time my children had to go to school, I had to find a relative to take them because I was forbidden to enter educational premises. When you are a mother, that first day in school for your child is one of the greatest things. It means so much both to you and to your child. I've never been able to do that. I am extremely sensitive about my children. They went to so many schools, it's a long, long story. They kept being expelled once it was discovered who they were – but they were toddlers, they knew nothing. People were petrified. For me just to find somebody who would register my child was something, because that meant this person would have a dossier opened at John Vorster Square.*And this is what happened. People were taken to John Vorster Square for having taken my children to school, and were interrogated.

The last one they were thrown out of was a Coloured school I had placed them at in desperation. Nelson's relative, the only person I could find to take them, couldn't register them at a black school, because she was Coloured – these were the Nationalists' laws. She could only take them to a Coloured school and register them in her name. And a Security Branch man called Van Tonder, who had a tough reputation, actually went to detain the school principal. Zindzi was then seven and Zeni eight years old. That's how I came to send them to Swaziland in 1967. Elinor Birley,† who was a friend of mine, took over arranging their education, together with Helen Joseph. They helped me so much in those years when I could do nothing. I didn't have a job, I spent

---

*Prison and headquarters of the Security Police where the notorious interrogations are conducted.

†Wife of Sir Robert Birley, former headmaster of Eton College and visiting Professor of Education at the University of the Witwatersrand.

most of my time in detention, I could not play my role as a parent. That's how they got admitted to Waterford School. Many times when the girls came home from school, they found the house locked and had to look in the newspaper to see if I was detained. The school principal would call them and say, 'Look, don't be disturbed when you see press reports that your mother is in detention again.' I never met a single one of those teachers in Waterford who did such a tremendous job teaching my children.

As some form of compensation you try to do everything you can for your children and perhaps even do too much, because you want to obliterate the fact in their minds that they haven't got a father and not only that, they haven't got maternal love when they need it. That is very hard for a mother, especially in a state of perpetual war where I cannot give them any kind of security. Our house was an extension of the police station, every day they came; the children were petrified. No amount of explanation could reassure them because I had no protection. Zindzi one day said, 'Are you really our mother? Maybe you are just a young girl Daddy hired to look after us.' She had seen photos of her father looking like a real father figure and here I was looking like a girl. That alone showed her insecurity.

At no time in their lives have they ever been sure whether they have either of their parents with them. They have grown up on their own, with friends. They knew we loved them but we were never there to express it – it was love by proxy.

It was not by choice that I spent so much time in prison but that did not stop me from having this enormous guilt that I had not played my role as a mother. You can't stop asking yourself what comes first, the nation or your children. We had chosen the nation.

I lost so many jobs at the time – a furniture shop, a dry-cleaning shop, a shoe-repair shop – they were countless. I was hired on a Monday and fired on a Friday. The Security Police went to each and every employer to intimidate them and to prevent my employment. One manager told me, 'You can keep this job for the rest of your life if you agree to divorce your husband.' That's what the police had told him.

I knew all the questions by heart and the last question was always: 'What about your political commitment?' Then it was the usual thing: 'Sorry, you qualify for the job, but your political views don't make it possible.'

So it was almost impossible to keep a job, and I was in constant danger of being sent to prison again. It is very difficult not to violate any of your banning orders at one time or another. Usually they would give you a long suspended sentence – in fact, that was worse than an ordinary sentence. In 1967 I got a suspended sentence of twelve months, of which I had to serve four days in jail. Something is bound to happen during that time and then you would be charged again for the same thing and the whole twelve months would come into effect anyhow.

But, according to Mandela, unjust laws are made to be defied.

I was heavily involved politically in the sixties, although I couldn't be so openly. We were re-conscientizing the youth, there were cells throughout the country – not communist cells! We established study groups and lectures on history to bring the youth up to date with the political thinking of the time and to keep in touch with them.

THE DAUGHTERS: ZINDZISWA AND ZENANI

'I have wonderful memories of my childhood,' says Zindzi, the youngest. When their mother was not there, there was always her brother or an uncle staying with them at the house who gave the children a sense of a family unit. And when she was there, the children felt 'incredibly spoilt', more with love than anything else. 'It might have been because she felt guilty that my father wasn't there and she felt she had to play the role of both parents.' The daughters remember the beautiful Xhosa lullabies their mother used to sing them in the evening. To the girls she is also a friend and a sister, 'If something crops up, we sit down and talk. She has always been so understanding. That's why I think she is also such a good social worker.' And they admire her as a granny too, how she would roll over the lawn with her grandchildren and toss them up in the air.

'Mummy has so many principles, I don't even know where to start,' says Zindzi. 'But she doesn't have double standards – she lives up to them. She even flushed all her heart tablets down the toilet, because she only believes in exercise and a healthy diet. She is such a health fanatic, she doesn't eat junk – that's how she manages to stay so young.

'She is very proud of her traditional music and dress; she is always in beads and kaftans. But she only dresses up for a reason, for instance when she has to appear in court. Around home she wears T-shirts and jeans. She loves military attire too; she's got a khaki outfit and men's boots and a beret. I think I will get her a toy gun and a holster for her to walk around and appear in court like that.

'She is a very sweet person, but when she gets into those fights with the police, it's bad, you know; she's got a hell of a temper.

'My mother has made us strong. Once in court, when Mummy was convicted – I think it was '71 – I started crying and outside court she said, "You must never cry, because you are giving them satisfaction if you do so."

'When you live with someone like my mother, you learn to live without fear. I'm totally immune to these people and their threats. I just go on with what I'm doing.

'Once, when Mummy had been permitted to come to Orlando for a weekend, the Security Police checked whether she had left in time for Brandfort. They stormed in – our dog attacked them and they started shooting – but I ignored them and just continued hanging up my washing. When they come now they just rattle at the door or throw stones on the roof. And when they make threatening or obscene phone calls, I just hang up.'

'If I get a phone call in Swaziland now,' says Zeni, 'telling us Mummy has been arrested, I say, "So what." But it was bad when we were younger. Most of my friends were really scared to visit me at home in Orlando. People have been picked up after visiting us. My husband helped me a lot because he wasn't scared to come to our home.'

When Winnie Mandela says that they should have the freedom of choosing whether they want to be committed to the cause – 'About the only freedom they have anyway' – Zindzi has chosen. 'I have suffered like every black child has, so I have a certain duty and role to play in my own society – independent of my being Mandela's daughter. I can't understand a black person who has suffered and who knows who is responsible and just sits back. I'm prepared to fight for my rights.'

She is proud of being a Mandela daughter – and sometimes it's even useful. 'In Soweto you can get into dangerous situations at night: when guys see girls coming up the road, they call, "Hey, you, come here"; then I say who I am and they immediately respect me – "Oh sorry". That always works when I'm in trouble. Or if I run out of money in a taxi and I say who I am, the driver lets me go and they always ask: "How is your father? How is Winnie, how is she coping?"

'I think my mother copes so well because she's got this tremendous hope and determination, and she knows she is not alone. People still regard her as a leader. They come all the way from Johannesburg to Brandfort to ask for her advice. She is incredible at bringing people together.

'She is going to get her liberation and she knows the people are on her side. I am very proud of her.'

LETTER* FROM NELSON MANDELA ON ROBBEN ISLAND TO WINNIE MANDELA

15.4.76

... As I woke up on the morning of 25 February I was missing you and the children a great deal as always. These days I spend quite some time thinking of you both as Dadewethu, Mum, pal and mentor. What you perhaps don't know is how I often think and actually picture in mind all that makes you up physically and spiritually – the loving remarks which came daily and the blind eye you've always turned against those numerous irritations that would have frustrated another woman. Sometimes it's a wonderful experience to ... think back about precious moments spent with you, darling. I even remember a day when you were bulging with Zindzi, struggling to cut your nails. I now recall those incidents with a sense of shame. I could have done it for you. Whether or not I was conscious of it, my attitude was: I've done my duty, a second brat is on the way, the difficulties you are now facing as a result of your physical condition are all yours. My only consolation is the knowledge that then I led a life where I'd hardly enough time even to think. Only I wonder what it'll be like when I return. But with you around, those to whom you mean so much ought to improve all the time.

... Good girl! At last you're back at Unisa.† What are your subjects? Do you still remember that you were at the same varsity when we met eighteen years ago? I hope you'll enjoy the course. But

---

*Letters from and to political prisoners were limited to 500 words and could only discuss personal and family matters.

†Correspondence university in Pretoria.

remember that I expect you to live up to the high standard I know you're capable of. But it really shook me to learn that in the evenings you drive to the Public Library. How can you take such a risk? Have you forgotten that you live in Soweto, not in the centre of town where you'd be safe at night? For the last decade you've been the object of cowardly night attempts on your life in which they tried to drag you out of the house. How can you now offer them such an ideal opportunity. Your life and that of the children is more important than an educational certificate. I hope in your next letter you'll tell me that you have dropped that, that after work you drive straight home and remain there with Zeni and the others till the next morning. Unisa and the State Library run a van service for reference books and you could make use of that.

I almost forgot to say that there're victories whose glory lies in the fact they're known only to those who win them, but there are wounds which leave deep scars when they heal. If on my return I found you away from home I'd seek you out and report to you first, for that honour is yours and yours alone.

Your beautiful photo still stands about two feet above my left shoulder as I write this note. I dust it carefully every morning, for to do so gives me the pleasant feeling that I'm caressing you as in the old days. I even touch your nose with mine to recapture the electric current that used to flush through my blood whenever I did so. Neolitha stands on the table directly opposite me. How can my spirits ever be down when I enjoy the fond attentions of such wonderful ladies . . .

I love you! Devotedly, Dalibunga

LETTER FROM NELSON MANDELA TO HIS DAUGHTER ZINDZI

4·9·77

Your disappointment with my brief letters is quite reasonable because it coincides with my own feelings when I get a stingy note or nothing at all from those I love. It pleases me to know that you're taking driving lessons and I hope you'll be as careful a driver as Mum is. Thembi* could drive the colossal Oldsmobile at ten. But if you

*Mandela's eldest son.

get your licence, you'll have done better than Mum and I. We were twenty-six and thirty-three respectively when we got ours. Good luck, darling!

I am also pleased to learn that you're a *True Love* columnist and that you have already received your first cheque. That's no small achievement at your age and it was very nice of JB to give you such a challenging opportunity. Writing is a prestigious profession which puts one right into the centre of the world and, to remain on top, one has to work really hard, the aim being a good and original theme, simplicity in expression and the use of the irreplaceable word. In this regard, you've many able friends who could help you. Benjie* is one of them. From your poem,† which is full of much promise, you have the markings of a professional in this field.

Brandfort becoming a nice place! I can't believe it. Mum has lost almost everything; she'll never get any job there except perhaps as domestic or farm hand or washerwoman; she'll spend all her days in poverty. She's described the sort of structure in which you must now live and the type of toilet and water facilities that you have to use. I fear to ask her the fortune she'll have to pay to make that place really fit to live in. You'll never eat or dress well as you did in JHB, nor will you be able to afford a TV set, see a decent film, go to a theatre or have a telephone.

Nonetheless, darling, I'm glad to note that you're adjusting yourself and trying to be happy all the same. I felt tremendous when I read the lines 'a nice place after all'. As long as you have an iron will, darling, you can turn misfortune into advantage, as you yourself say. Were it not so, Mum would have been a complete wreck by now.

[About the boyfriend.] Such relations are confidential and ought not to be discussed through letters. For one thing, I don't have all the information I need to give you proper advice. But in our present circs. that's a difficulty we can't altogether avoid. Seldom in life does one find a perfect boy- or girl-friend. Normally, it's sufficient that the two are sincerely in love, and the rest is a question of mutual understanding and influence. Frank but tactful discussions might clear away delicate problems.

One Saturday after 1 p.m. and about a month before Mum and I got married, she came with friends to fetch me from the office and found me waiting for the secretary of a foreign statesman with whom

---

*Benjamin Pogrond, Foreign Editor of the *Rand Daily Mail*.
† A collection of Zindzi's poems, *Black As I Am*, was published in California in 1978.

I had an appointment. Like Mum, she was shatteringly beautiful and about the same age and, although they'd not met, Mum was at once surprisingly hostile. Then I was in top physical condition and going to the gym regularly. In spite of all that, and in the presence of others, she caught me by the the scruff of the neck and dragged me out. I never saw that lady again ...

Today we've a high-souled and tolerant family shepherdess who has made a man of me.

If, in spite of your best efforts, you feel that there's no real improvement in your relations, then you must not at all hesitate to end them. One thing you must never do is to allow anybody, no matter who he is, how deeply you may love him, to bully you. I'd be very disappointed if that happened. To the best of my recollection, I've never tried that either with Mum or with any of my children. We have chatted on problems as equals and I won't tolerate anybody who tries that to you. Does that ease your own problems a bit?

Mum would collapse if you got married now. You're the last straw to which she now clings and her happiness is very much in your hands. Priority No. 1, I repeat, priority No. 1 is your studies, you must certainly take your English scholarship at all costs. That's what Mum and I would love to see.

There are moments in life when people forget their precious gifts as human beings, virtues that make them shine wherever they may be and whatever the difficulties; times when those who're always sure of themselves begin to hesitate, when potential geniuses look less than average, when something caves in and an otherwise tough and dynamic person melts into soft and motionless jelly jammed down by the walls of its container. They mean this when they say life is no bed of roses.

No Human Being Can Go on Taking Those Humiliations without Reaction

IN PRISON

'I got more liberated in prison. The physical identification with your beliefs is far more satisfying than articulating them on a platform. I am not saying it is best to be in prison. But under the circumstances, where it is a question of which prison is better, the prison outside or inside – the whole country is a prison for the black man – and when you are inside, you know why you are there and the people who put you there also know.

DETENTION AND TRIAL, 1969

In May 1969 Winnie Mandela and twenty-one men and women were detained in nationwide dawn raids under the Terrorism Act. She was to spend 491 days in detention, most of it in solitary confinement. They were then charged under the Suppression of Communism Act with 'furthering the aims of an unlawful organization' and the state alleged that 'the accused acted in concert and with a common purpose to re-establish and build up the ANC, knowing that its ultimate aim was the violent overthrow of the state'. The ninety-nine counts ranged from giving the ANC salute, singing ANC songs, recruiting members, discussing or possessing ANC literature, to 'polluting' the youth.

The evidence of state witnesses was unconvincing; it became obvious that they had been tortured and forced to make incriminating statements. The state withdrew all the charges, and on 16 February 1970 Winnie Mandela and the other defendants were all acquitted.

As they prepared to leave the court, they were re-detained, under Section 6 of the Terrorism Act. Not until June, and only after widespread protests, were Mrs Mandela and nineteen others finally charged under that Act. Almost all the charges were repetitions of those on which they had already been acquitted. Again, on 14 September 1970, they were all acquitted.

Within two weeks Winnie Mandela was served with a new, five-year banning order restricting her to Orlando West and placing her under house arrest each night and during weekends and public holidays. She was served with the new bans just as she was leaving for Robben Island to visit her husband, whom she had not seen for two years.

In the years that followed there were frequent attacks on her life and property: on one occasion a gunman was found in her yard, on another her house was broken into; a petrol bomb was hurled through a window; her watchdog was poisoned; and one night three men broke in and attempted to strangle her. Her daughter Zindzi appealed to the United Nations to call on the South African Government to protect her mother.

IN PRISON

I was detained on 12 May 1969. Detention means that midnight knock when all about you is quiet. It means those blinding torches shone simultaneously through every window of your house before the door is kicked open. It means the exclusive right the Security Branch have to read each and every letter in the house. It means paging through each and every book on your shelves, lifting carpets, looking under beds, lifting sleeping children from mattresses and looking under the sheets. It means tasting your sugar, your mealie-meal and every spice on your kitchen shelf. Unpacking all your clothing and going through each pocket. Ultimately it means your seizure at dawn, dragged away from little children screaming and clinging to your skirt, imploring the white man dragging Mummy away to leave her alone.

We were the first prisoners under Section 6 of the Terrorism Act.* I was kept in Pretoria Central Prison. My cell had a grille inside, a door in the middle and another grille outside. From what I heard and had

---

*The Terrorism Act, No. 83 of 1967, empowers the South African police to arrest any person suspected of committing acts endangering the maintenance of law and order or conspiring or inciting people to commit such acts. The Act is so loosely defined that almost any opponent of the South African regime can be arrested without a warrant, detained for interrogation and kept in solitary confinement without access to a lawyer or relative for an indefinite period of time. Children are not exempted.

read I realized that mine must be the death cell. I did not even know I was with other detainees in the same block. I thought I was alone; for months I didn't know that the whole country had been rounded up. All I could hear was a distant cough and a faint sound of prison doors being locked.

Those first few days are the worst in anyone's life – that uncertainty, that insecurity: there is such a sense of hopelessness, the feeling that this is now the end. The whole thing is calculated to destroy you, not only morally but also physically. You knew the enemy could keep you there for five years. You are not in touch with anybody. And in those days all I had in the cell was a sanitary bucket, a plastic bottle which could contain only about three glasses of water, and a mug.

Sometimes they would bring a little plastic bucket with water to wash yourself, but you didn't get any water to wash your clothes. They must have been sanitary buckets because the smell was terrible. They weren't even properly rinsed. So I used the drinking water from the plastic bottle to wash my face. And I had to use my panties to wash my body because there was nothing else. During menstruation we only got toilet paper or they would say, 'Go and use your big fat hands.' For a bed there was only a mat and three stinking filthy blankets. I rolled one up for a pillow and slept with the other two.

The days and nights became so long I found I was talking to myself. It is deathly quiet – that alone is a torture. You don't know what to do with yourself; you sit down, you stand up, you pace up and down. The cell is so small that you can't even run right round. You lie on your stomach, you lie on your back, on your side; your body becomes sore, because you are not used to sleeping on cement. What kept me going in the cells were the Canadian Air Force exercises for women – I'm addicted to those, I couldn't live without them.

You find yourself looking for anything in the cells; for instance, I remember how happy I was when I found two ants, how I spent the whole day with these ants, playing with them on my finger and how sad I was when the warders switched off the light. That was during the day, but the building was so old that it was perpetually dark. Then there was nothing else to do. So I started ripping one of those blankets, pulling out the threads and making little ropes. I spent whole days making them and undoing them. Then I undid the hem of my dress, just to have something to do. After that there was nothing else to do.

At night it was not possible to sleep. They kept the light on, but also I had been suffering from acute insomnia for some years. During interrogation through the night Swanepoel* referred to that and said, 'We are providing company for you all night long and you are ungrateful.'

We had inspection every day in prison. Two wardresses walk in, they order you to stand up, they take off your clothes. They start by inspecting your shoes as you stand there stark naked. They go through your panties, your bra, they go through every seam of every garment. Then they go through your hair and – of course, they never succeeded with me, but with female prisoners it's common practice – they inspect the vagina. I don't think they did that to my other five comrades who were also in that prison. Nothing is more humiliating. And you are all alone in that cell.

When I got permission to get a few clothes from relatives, the process now took twice the amount of time.

I was so angry. I considered just about everything I could do to myself as a form of protest. If I didn't have children, and if it wasn't for the fact that I would be playing into the authorities' hands, I might have taken my life. But one would be doing this for people who have no conscience at all.

My interrogation started on a Monday. And I was only delivered back to the cell on the Saturday night. They interrogated me for five days and five nights. I remember that vaguely. During the fifth night I was having these fainting spells which are very relieving. It was the first time I realized that nature has a fantastic way of providing for excess exhaustion of the body. I just had these long blackouts; I must have been delivered back in the cell during one of them. We were interrogated continuously. My whole body was badly swollen, I was passing blood. There were times when one was allowed to go to the toilet, but very briefly, and a woman wardress would actually go into the toilet with you.

They do give you something to eat, but you can't eat under those

---

*One of the most notorious members of the Security Police; a number of detainees interrogated by him alleged torture.

circumstances – food is of no relevance. The whole experience is so terrible, because I had left little children at home in bed and I had no idea what had happened to them.

The interrogation was about the activities of the banned African National Congress, and the 'communist' contacts we were supposed to have outside. Of course, a lot of activities had been taking place, activities which in a democratic country are everyone's rights. We had informal education groups and meetings, which take place in every country. There was nothing illegal about that. Rita Ndzanga and I were interrogated when they were almost through with the others who had been rounded up. She and I were both banned people, so we had naturally been using contacts. I was interrogated for hours about some women we had been helping – they were members of the South African Federation of Women who had been in prison since 1960. These women had not had visitors – the old tactic, when people were tucked away in prison, and families were not told which prison they were in.

We had tried to find out where they were being held, and we sent our women there to pose as relatives to be able to bring them basic necessities like soap and toothpaste and toilet-paper – little things that make life in prison a little easier, which they hadn't seen for years. Where a visit was not possible, we sent postal orders in the name of their relatives. With the help of the Anglican Church we collected money for their families to make sure that the imprisoned women's rent could be paid in their absence. It was a welfare service which would have been normal and legal in any other country.

But in this insane society it had to be clandestine. During interrogation they insisted it was a communist-inspired type of thing, and that we were trying to convey secret messages underground. Rita was tortured very badly, she nearly died.

We were interrogated by Swanepoel. He said some of the most extraordinary things to me during interrogation: 'You are going to be broken completely, you are shattered, you are a finished woman.' And: 'You know, people think Nelson is a great man, they think he is in prison because he wanted to sacrifice for his people. If I had a wife like you, I would do exactly what Nelson has done and go and seek protection in prison. He ran away from you. What kind of woman holds meetings up till four o'clock in the morning with other people's husbands? You are the only woman who does this kind of thing.'

And then he presented me with statements they claimed to have extracted from these men: alleged meetings with five or six of them in Nelson's bedroom.

Those were horrible days. I hate to recall them. And I was already quite sick when I went to prison. I hadn't been able to sleep at all and in prison it was the same; sometimes I wasn't able to sleep for twenty-four hours. To have something to do, I started scraping off the paint from the wall with my finger-nails and at one stage I found underneath the paint an inscription which I could read quite clearly: 'Mrs Mandela is a sell-out.'

And then Swanepoel asked, 'What do you think you are resisting? You are politically naked.' That I was stripped of every friend in the struggle. He said: 'We have succeeded in telling people that you want to work for us, it hardly makes a difference to us whether you want to work for us or not. Do you want to work for us, so that we release you from prison?'

I would have come out in the very first month of those seventeen months in solitary confinement if I had agreed to the ludicrous suggestions that were made: that if I co-operated and allowed my voice to be used over the air to call upon our ANC forces at the border to retreat and put down their arms and have discussions with the government, I would be released. I was actually going to be flown by helicopter to see Nelson – with top-ranking police officers – to hold secret discussions with Nelson on the island, and after that he would be removed from the other prisoners and put into the cottage where the late Robert Sobukwe was held on the island. My husband would suffer more comfortably. They never gave up – right through my detention. That's how narrow-minded these people can be. After you've given the best years of your life to this cause – that they can dream that your principles can still be for sale! If there weren't people in this country who would still fight for justice, my fate would have been the same as that of most blacks in this land. Most blacks in this country go to jail for nothing: thousands are arrested every day whose only offence is wanting to live together as a family. I was lucky to have lawyers for my defence who have done everything to prove my innocence in court.

I forgot to say I had the Bible, because it was such a meaningless document in those circumstances. I read it four times. I never knew it was possible to read the Bible from beginning to end.

What was so ironical – we know how religious Afrikaners want to appear. Well, the way I got the Bible in prison – one of the Security men stood at the entrance, the door was flung open and he threw the Bible at my feet – 'There is the Bible, ask your God to release you from jail!'

Even for people who are not very religious, the Bible still inspires some form of respect. Now here are people who are supposed to be religious mocking this same God who they believe predestined them to be the rulers of this country. When they oppress us, they oppress us in God's name, they call themselves God's chosen people. In the name of *that* God he flung that Bible at me, and yet he stands in the pulpit every Sunday to preach what he has never believed in. The Security Police are a special breed. In order to belong you have to have this particular hatred of the black man. Otherwise how would you torture people to death for ideological differences, how would you point a machine gun at a seven-year-old child and blast his brains out? You have to be of a special breed, one I know well, which has made my life impossible. And they are the people who have taught me to hate.

I'm not saying every Afrikaner is like that; I'm saying the Afrikaner who oppresses my people is like that. They are petrified of the black man, so much so that they actually become prisoners themselves. Look at those wardresses in prison: they are really worse prisoners than us, wearing that sordid uniform and standing for hours over us – what type of person goes for that job? And once you try to communicate with them through English, they see red. These girls don't know a word in English, not even a greeting. And which political prisoner would speak Afrikaans in prison! So there is just no level of communication, only a total breakdown.

They didn't let black warders come near us – we had only white warders and wardresses.

When they brought our food in the morning, it was porridge. That was how we knew it was morning. They would take the sanitary buckets and bring them back without even rinsing them, turn the lid upside down, put the plate of food on that lid and you would just see a white leg pushing in that sanitary bucket.

It was impossible to eat. They used to put the plates of food outside next to the cells and by the time it came, it was full of bird shit – besides the porridge was uncooked.

We didn't get the same food as Coloured prisoners and the Indians. They get coffee, tea, bread and sugar. 'Bantu' get porridge without sugar, and something pitch black with lumps in it supposed to be coffee.

Lunch was supposed to be better, but the spinach and carrots were just as they were from the garden, unwashed, impossible to swallow. For supper we had porridge again which often floated in blood. They must have cooked meat in the pot. So we went on a hunger strike for a week, although it was difficult to communicate. We did it by banging on the wall.

We tried to raise complaints with the doctors but they would just rush through, looking briefly inside, shouting '*Klagte?*' ['Any complaints?'], and by the time you are supposed to reply, he is already ten paces away.

I suffered from malnutrition; the complexion becomes sallow, you get bleeding gums from lack of vitamins; I could not stand, I had fever and blackouts. When we were to be charged in October, I could not appear in court. I had to be taken to the prison hospital.

The only time we had some relief was when our complaints were raised in court by our lawyers. George Bizos had to apply to court for us to have baths – up to that date we hadn't been showering or washing.

There was no improvement in the prison food as a result of the hunger strike, but at least we got our food from relatives. They never stopped trying to humiliate us. When we prepared for the court case, my family brought me some clothes. When we came back to our cells after consulting with our attorneys, not only had they emptied the suitcase on the floor but they had opened jars of cosmetics and thrown them on the clothes. There was cream all over and muddy footprints. I had no way of washing or ironing them! I stood there at the door – then came the stripping, the usual process – and when I saw the woman in charge of the prison, I was so angry I saw red, the same as I had when that policeman came to my bedroom. I don't know how she escaped that cell. No human being can go on taking those humiliations without reaction.

You cannot intimidate people like me any more. In 1974 when I was convicted and was serving six months in Kroonstad Prison, I met one of our symbols of resistance, Dorothy Nyembe,* a close friend of Nelson's. To be there with a woman who was serving fifteen years as she was, who was as courageous as she was, was a tremendous experience for me. She is a devout Christian. The determination in her! She was already over fifty when I met her. I found her a solid pillar of strength. She had been in prison since 1968, but she was so undaunted. Her spirit was exactly the same as when she went in. She is one of the old heroes, one of the great women who have personally made me what I am.

I got more liberated in prison. The physical identification with your beliefs is far more satisfying than articulating them on a platform. My soul has been more purified by prison than anything else. I am not saying it is best to be in prison. But under the circumstances, where it is a question of which prison is better, the prison outside or inside – the whole country is a prison for the black man – and when you are inside, you know why you are there, and the people who put you there also know.

A FELLOW PRISONER ON WINNIE MANDELA

Rita Ndzanga, herself actively engaged for many years in political work with women and the trade unions, was also detained from May 1969 in Pretoria Central Prison:

I didn't even know that Winnie was also arrested. I only knew that my husband and myself were picked up. When I got there I realized that Winnie was also in. There was a big filing cabinet, and written on it was 'Operation Winnie Mandela'.

We had a bad time under the white wardresses. They used to hate us, especially Winnie. She wouldn't let them hit the other prisoners, she even wrote reports about the hittings and gave them to the lawyers.

One day a certain brigadier tried to manhandle a woman, Martha Dlamini; she was over fifty. And Winnie got up and said, 'You dare touch her, you dare touch that woman!' The man just ran back, because Winnie was at the door. Then he said, 'I'm going to give you a hiding.'

*One of South Africa's longest-serving female political prisoners, sentenced for harbouring guerrillas of Umkhonto we Sizwe; she was released from prison on 26 March 1984.

And I told him, 'Just now you said you were going to give Winnie a hiding. Winnie is my leader's wife, you've got to apologize. I am not going to have my leader's wife spoken to in that way.' He just kept quiet. Afterwards the matrons were so furious! There were about three of them, reprimanding Winnie, waving sticks. 'If you speak like that again you are going to get this.' And Winnie said, 'You just try, you bloody old cows!' She's a courageous woman, a brave woman, outspoken and very fearless. And a wonderful personality, too. Independent of her husband – she's a leader in herself. Despite the fact that they took her to Brandfort, she is still the same in our people's hearts.

HARASSED, BANNED, DETAINED

CHARGES AGAINST WINNIE MANDELA AND COURT CASES

1958 Arrested for participation in the women's demonstration in Johannesburg against the issuing of passes to women. Imprisoned for two weeks.

1962 Banned for two years under the Suppression of Communism Act. Restricted to Johannesburg.

1963 Arrested for attending a gathering; found not guilty and acquitted.

1965 A more stringent banning order for five years and restriction to Orlando township. As a result she lost her job with the Child Welfare Society.

1966 Additional restrictions imposed, prohibiting her from 'preparing, compiling, publishing, printing or transmitting any document, book, pamphlet, record, poster, photograph', etc. etc. Accused of violating regulations for visit to Robben Island – instead of going by train she had gone by plane to get there before her permit expired.

1967 Accused of resisting arrest; during a scuffle a policeman broke his neck (it was not fatal); she was found not guilty and was acquitted.

1967	Accused of violating her banning order: failed to give her name and address to the Security Police in Cape Town. Sentence: twelve months' imprisonment suspended for three years; she had spent four days in prison.
1969	Detained (with twenty-one others) under the Suppression of Communism Act and accused of having promoted the aims of the banned ANC. As a result she lost her job. Charges withdrawn in February 1970.
1970	Immediately re-detained in solitary confinement under Section 6 of the Terrorism Act with virtually the same charges; acquitted in September 1970. Two weeks unbanned.
1970	Banning order renewed for five years, plus house arrest each night and during weekends – visitors forbidden.
1970	Accused of violating her banning order by receiving visitors – five relatives (two of them children) who called at her house. Sentence: six months' imprisonment suspended for three years, this was set aside on appeal.
1971	Accused of violating her banning order: communication with a banned person in her house (Peter Magubane). Sentence: twelve months' imprisonment suspended for three years. Conviction and sentence were set aside on appeal.
1973	Accused of violating her banning order: lunch with her children in a Combi in the presence of a banned person (Peter Magubane). Sentence: twelve months' imprisonment suspended for three years.
1974	On appeal in October 1974 sentence was reduced to six months, which she served in Kroonstad Prison.
1975	Third banning order expired; ten months' 'freedom' (after thirteen years of banning).
1976	Detained on 12 August under Section 6 of the Internal Security Act after the Soweto uprising; imprisoned in the 'Fort' in Johannesburg until December 1976.
1977	Banning order renewed for five years.

1977   Banished to Brandfort in the Orange Free State on 17 May.

1977–9   Countless arrests in Brandfort because of violations of her banning order; almost daily, sometimes twice daily. She refuses to keep 'such a despicable statistic'.

1978   Court case on alleged incitement of the Soweto uprising; acquitted and awarded compensation for defamation.

1980   Accused of assaulting a policeman while in Johannesburg; found not guilty and acquitted.

1980   Accused of violating her banning order by having a friend of the family as a lodger in her house in Brandfort; case postponed.

1982   Banning order renewed for another five years.

1982–5   Numerous charges in connection with violations of her banning order, but few were brought to court.

According to the banning order, served on her by the Minister of Justice for the first time in 1962 under section 10(1)(a) of the Suppression of Communism Act, No. 44 of 1950, Winnie Mandela was required to abstain from any activity which might spread or promote any of the objects of 'communism' in South Africa. 'Receiving visitors' and having 'social intercourse', for instance, are part of the long list of prohibitions contained in the documents, in order to prevent the creation of an opportunity to 'clandestinely conspire to engage in communist activities'.

In South Africa it is illegal to quote a banned person.

Each case involves hair-splitting sophistry and the consultation of a whole range of dictionaries to interpret in which context a 'visitor', a 'gathering' or a conversation is deemed to be 'legal' or 'illegal'.

A few examples from the court records show the absurdity of some of the cases – the absurdity of life itself under a banning order. In most cases the sentence was set aside on appeal.

In the Regional Court in Johannesburg Winnie Mandela was accused of having received five visitors on 2 October 1970: her sister Nobantu Mniki with her husband and their two children, as well as her brother-in-law Gilbert Xaba, who came to fetch a shopping list at her house at 8115

Orlando. Winnie Mandela, 'an adult Bantu female', was sentenced to six months' imprisonment suspended for three years.

In terms of her banning/house-arrest order under the Suppression of Communism Act she was prohibited from 'receiving any visitors' other than her doctor and her children. On appeal, the State Prosecutor contended that the words 'receive' and 'visitor' must be given their 'ordinary, literary, grammatical meaning'. Advocate George Bizos, the defence counsel, insisted that the words 'receive' and 'visitor' should be given a restricted meaning as in previous cases. The proper meaning to be given to 'receive' was 'to give shelter or harbour' and a 'visitor' was a 'person who stays with one for a period of time as a guest'. The defence maintained that 'members of the family who casually came to appellant's residence could not be said to have been received as "visitors" if their stay was brief and unimportant as in the case of Xaba and Mniki'. According to that logic, a 'business call' like that of Xaba would fall outside the scope of the prohibition, as would the 'visits' of the milk-delivery man, the postman, the refuse collector, the light- and water-meter reader and the like. Otherwise, even the policeman checking her movements in and out of her house would be prohibited.

Bizos said the interpretation of the order should be restricted to its original purpose, i.e. to isolate the addressee, thereby preventing clandestine collaboration in promoting 'communist activities'. By no stretch of the imagination could the presence of a nine-month-old baby and a two-and-a-half-year-old toddler be seen as endangering the security of the state, nor could they conspire to form an illegal organization. Besides, there was no evidence that, while Mrs Mniki was in the house, the appellant had spoken to her; nor was there evidence that she stayed in the same room with the visitors all the time.

The sentence was set aside on appeal.

The scope of interpretation as to whether a person 'advocates, advises, defends or encourages the achievement of any of the objects of communism' can be seen from the following court case.

On 9 July 1967 the accused did not report to the Security Police on her arrival in Cape Town and 'wrongfully and unlawfully' failed to furnish her name and address to a Sergeant Sekame of the South Africa police.

According to court records, the story can be summarized as follows. After the appellant had visited her husband on Robben Island on 9 July 1967 she returned by boat to the mainland at about 4.30 p.m. When she disembarked,

Sergeant Sekame asked her where she was living in Cape Town. He says that she responded: 'What for? It is your duty to find the whereabouts of Mrs Mandela; if you are a policeman, you should know my address. I don't give my address to strangers.' He then demanded her address. She replied: 'It is your way of getting an earning to trace where I am staying. Leave me alone and stand out of my way.' She then walked towards the car and drove off to Cape Town. Sekame said that she was very cross at the time.

Whereas Sekame maintained that he had informed her that he was a policeman, the appellant said that she thought Sekame was a reporter. The magistrate in the lower court had accepted the evidence of Sekame, and Mrs Mandela was convicted to twelve months' imprisonment, of which all but four days were suspended for three years. On appeal the defence contended that, as she was merely staying in Cape Town for two days at an address in Nyanga, it could not be said that she had an 'address' in Cape Town. The state argued that she did have an 'address', which, according to Webster's Dictionary, third edition, is 'a place where [she] can be found and communicated with', and that she had deliberately refused to give it to the officer. Her appeal was dismissed and the conviction and sentence confirmed. She had to spend four days in prison.

Another contravention of her banning order, for which she had to serve six months in prison, was the alleged communication with another banned person, Peter Magubane, on 10 May 1973. For the following incident they were sentenced to twelve months' imprisonment each: Peter Magubane had brought the two young daughters of Winnie Mandela in a Combi to a point near her place of her employment, so that they could meet. The children had come from boarding school in Swaziland and it was only during school holidays that the mother was able to see them during her lunch hour.

The question whether this meeting was an illegal 'direct' communication between two banned persons or an 'indirect' communication via the children fills many pages in the court records.

The magistrate had convicted her as well as Peter Magubane in the lower court because the appellants must have communicated with each other through the children as intermediaries, since 'as long as something, however unimportant, passes from mind to mind, there is communication'. For the judge on appeal, however, it was 'quite conceivable' that the children were acting on their own behalf in requesting Magubane to convey them to various places in town to meet their mother. The original sentences of twelve months were reduced to six months in respect of each appellant. Winnie Mandela served six months in Kroonstad Prison.

We Couldn't Stop Our Children

THE SOWETO UPRISING, 1976

'The determination, the thirst for freedom in little children's hearts was such that they were prepared to face machine guns with stones. That is what happens when you want to break those chains of oppression. Nothing else seems to matter.'

THE BACKGROUND

On the morning of Wednesday 16 June 1976, 20,000 Soweto schoolchildren marched in protest against the government's order that Afrikaans must be used as a language of instruction in black secondary schools. They were said to be good-humoured and excited. Some carried placards with slogans: DOWN WITH AFRIKAANS! WE ARE NOT BOERS! IF WE MUST DO AFRIKAANS, VORSTER MUST DO ZULU.

Police vehicles raced to the scene and, when police tried to stop the march, students taunted them. Some said stones were thrown, others that stones were thrown only after the police opened fire. What is not contested is that police shot dead a thirteen-year-old boy, Hector Petersen, from behind, and killed several other people. Riots swept Soweto and, as police and army moved in in force and the deaths of children multiplied, black communities throughout the country similarly vented their fury by burning schools, Bantu Administration buildings, state-owned beer-halls and vehicles. Police

1   At Hector Peterson's funeral, the first victim of
the Soweto riots, 1976

2

2 Winnie Mandela banished to Brandfort, 1977

3 Winnie and her daughter Zindzi awaiting
   banishment to Brandfort, 1977

4 Brandfort black township

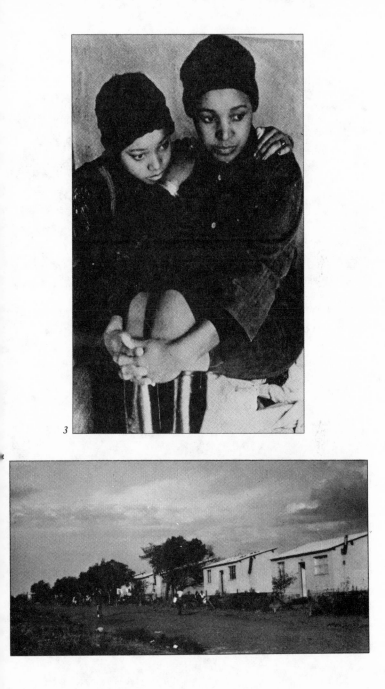

3

5 Winnie and her crèche in Brandfort, 1984
6 Women in Brandfort sewing school uniforms, 1984

7   Winnie in Orlando writing to Nelson, 1975
8   Winnie Mandela and Sally Motlana at the
        formation of the Black Women's Federation, 1975

9

9   Winnie and Nelson Mandela, 1959
10 Nelson Mandela
11 Winnie in traditional dress in Brandfort, 1978

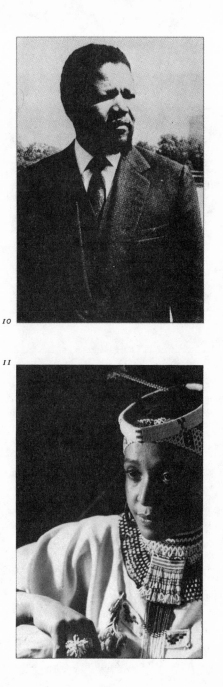

10

11

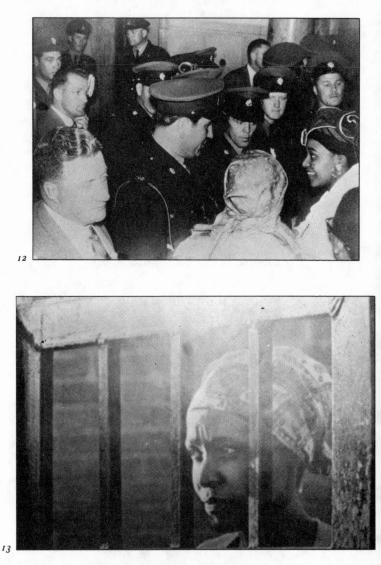

12   Winnie in front of Palace of Justice, 1962 at
        Nelson Mandela's trial

13   Winnie in Orlando behind the garden gate, 1969

stations and the homes of black policemen were attacked. Everywhere schools were boycotted.

The school students' uprising has to be seen within the context of Black Consciousness, the political movement founded in the early seventies by university students led by Steve Biko.* Its organizations filled the vacuum caused by the outlawing of the ANC and the PAC, and in their turn were all banned. Psychological liberation and pride in being black were essential to this movement which helped to spark off the 1976 protests; the Afrikaans language became the focus for the deep-seated bitterness at influx control, forced removals, inferior education, shortage of housing, police terror and denial of political rights.

It will never be known how many were killed in the uprising. The SA Institute of Race Relations estimated 618 killed and 1,500 injured –.most of them school students; to judge from Press reports the figures were much higher. By June 1977, of 21,534 prosecuted for such alleged offences as public violence, rioting, sabotage, incitement and arson, 13,553 had been convicted, nearly 5,000 of them under eighteen. An unknown number fled the country for military training or to obtain a proper education. The majority joined the ANC in exile. Oliver Tambo, who had left South Africa after Sharpeville in 1960 to set up missions and training bases abroad, was now ANC President General. Sabotage raids and attacks on police and defence installations by Umkhonto cadres marked a new phase in the struggle.

THE SOWETO UPRISING

In June 1976 the anger of young blacks in South Africa against the injustices of the regime had reached boiling point.

Twenty thousand children marched with slogans attacking Bantu Education and demanding the release of Mandela, Sisulu, and other political prisoners. The lessons of 1976 are there for anybody to see: here were children who ought to think of Mandela as a myth, who ought to think of him as somebody of the past. But they were singing about our leaders on Robben Island. They recognized a leadership that has been incarcerated for nearly twenty years.

*In September 1977 Biko became the fortieth detainee to die while in police custody.

June 1976, known as the 'uprising of Soweto', was a spontaneous flare-up of the country. No one organized it. The eruption on 16 June was an escalation of what had been simmering for weeks already. In May there had been open talk amongst the kids of taking action on the issue of Afrikaans in their schools: they had long been angry about this.

I was there among them, I saw what happened. The children picked up stones, they used dustbin lids as shields and marched towards machine guns. It's not that they don't know that the white man is heavily armed; they marched against heavy machine gun fire. You could smell gunfire everywhere. Children were dying in the street, and as they were dying, the others marched forward, facing guns. No one has ever underestimated the power of the enemy. We know that he is armed to the teeth. But the determination, the thirst for freedom in children's hearts, was such that they were prepared to face those machine guns with stones. That is what happens when you hunger for freedom, when you want to break those chains of oppression. Nothing else seems to matter.

We couldn't stop our children. We couldn't keep them off the streets. On 17 June – one day after hundreds of them had been shot in Soweto, we established the Black Parents Association (BPA).

We found ourselves in the middle of the conflict. The students demanded that we negotiate with Kruger, then Minister of Police. It was a mandate from the students who told us: 'If you want us to stop, go and tell Kruger our grievances.'

I was actually happy that Kruger refused to see us; he couldn't have done anything better. I was hoping he would refuse because it would have put our credibility at stake. Of course we wanted the bloodshed to stop, we didn't believe that our students should be cannon fodder; on the other hand, we had their mandate to negotiate. They would have felt we had let them down by not going. In that emotional atmosphere you could not argue. So Kruger saved us a lot by refusing.

In the Black Parents Association we had people from all schools of thought – religious leaders, social workers, different views from ours. I worked closely with Dr Motlana, Dr Mathlare and Bishop Buthelezi, our chairman.

In the BPA the children saw a mouthpiece, and the system automatically recognized it as their mouthpiece, although we were more active as a welfare organization. We raised money and organized mass burials, since hundreds of families didn't have any funds. Families had to be fed; there were orphans, who sometimes had only a grandmother left, who had to be taken care of. It was most painful when the authorities impounded something like R194,000 which had been donated for the victims.

The only time we ever saw any authority on the other side was when we went to Protea police station to plead that they should refrain from shooting at demonstrating children. As we entered, this Major Visser said something like this: 'You organized the riots, and now that they are out of control, you come to us. You know that you, Winnie Mandela, are entirely responsible for this.' There was the usual flare-up. I don't think Bishop Buthelezi had ever seen anything like that in his life. I wanted to restrain myself because of him but it was difficult.

We could not direct the students' activities, that was not our duty. But when we launched the BPA in May, I had addressed the Afrikaans issue: 'We must not let the children fight their battle for us, they must have our support,' I said. 'What the children learn in school is also our responsibility. If we let them down now, they will spit on our graves one day.'

The system maintained that I was manipulating and directing the struggle of the children. The whole reason behind all this was to discredit one politically, to show that the ANC spearheaded the uprising and that this was the quality of leadership that was involved. The same old story of agitators!

DR NTHATHO MOTLANA ADDS A NOTE ON THE BPA

For a long time there has been this awful schism between the PAC, the Black Consciousness Movement and the ANC. When we founded the Black Parents Association we needed to form an organization that could bridge the gap.

The youth, many of whom came under the influence of Black Consciousness, related very well to Winnie Mandela; they never had problems accepting Winnie's leadership, she transcends these differences. They go to her from all over. So in the BPA we needed the kind of role Winnie can play, her ability to bridge the gap between the youth and the adults and the different ideological factions.

As the only woman on the executive, she was more than a man; Winnie is powerful; she is faithful and honest. But above all, she is brave; she has got the kind of guts I don't have, many of us don't have. She would stand before police captains with machine guns and tell them to go and get stuffed. In fact, she used to scare us; often I would say, you are bloody foolhardy, you are going to get us all locked up, and when they threatened to lock her up she just said, 'Do it, man!'

When this Major Visser in Protea police station said to her that she had started the riots, she threw a book at him, her shoe, anything and everything she could lay her hands on – 'You bloody murderer, killer of our children, and you tell us *we* started the riots. You go and stop those bastards killing our children in the street!'

She is not scared of anything! We used to go in and out of those offices protesting against the killings and the police brutalities before we were all detained.

FEMALE SECTION IN THE 'FORT' IN JOHANNESBURG, 1976

In August 1976, in the aftermath of the Soweto uprising, Winnie Mandela (prisoner no. 4275/76) was imprisoned with a dozen other women in the 'Fort' in Johannesburg. Sally Motlana was one of them:

Winnie was a pillar of strength to most of us political detainees, and very sympathetic to the other prisoners. We were political prisoners under Section 10 and the other prisoners came to clean the yard and the *stoep*. They were not allowed to wear panties, they were not given any shoes and stockings, and she stood up for those poor women. She was really at loggerheads with the lieutenant herself, who was the top woman in that prison, saying that these people are not animals, they are human beings, and even if they are in jail they still want their dignity and you cannot strip them like that. After a week they were given shoes and stockings and panties. She was just out and out to fight for the underdog.

Our cells opened onto a yard. One day in my cell there was a broken window pane. I complained about this draught the very week I arrived. They didn't bother about that. So one day at half past three – our dinner was always at 3 p.m. – we were told to go into the cells. I pulled out my mattress and my blanket and went into my bed. So the wardress came and said, 'You have to go into that cell' and I said, 'Never! I'm not going back to that cell until that window is repaired. There is no difference between my sleeping inside that cell and outside.'

So Winnie said to the other girls, 'As long as she is not in, we are not going in either.' So the whole thirteen of us stayed outside. The wardress had to fetch the lieutenant and we were all singing and we said, 'We won't go in until that window pane is fixed.'

The lieutenant said, 'I promise you, tomorrow morning at seven, that window pane will be repaired.'

If Winnie hadn't organized the girls to stand together for this protest, they would have forced me somehow to go back. The next morning we saw men entering our courtyard, at a quarter to seven. How many? Six of them! To repair a small window pane!

Then the Red Cross visited us, and before they came there was so much spring cleaning – all of a sudden we were issued with prison linen, prison blankets and even bedspreads. I don't know whether they thought we would keep quiet and not tell the Red Cross people that normally we slept on the floor and this is just window dressing. They suddenly brought half a dozen flower-pots. So Winnie said: 'Flowers? We are not allowed to have flowers here. You'd better ask for permission first.' And the prison officials were so embarrassed.

Despite the hardships in her life – right through her married life, in the family and in the community – she was forever ready to listen, to smile, to comfort. To me a leader of that nature is a great leader. She would listen even to the smallest of us, and act. If you needed help in a difficult political situation, she knew which lawyers to go to, and she would actually drive you there. Or if you got into trouble with the Pass Laws, anything – she wouldn't say, how much is it going to cost me to go to town to help this woman. She would jump into her car and take you to a person who could give immediate help. I have worked with many leaders. Some are very self-assertive. But that girl was motherly, down to earth. To the young, to the old, she was the same.

The Chapter of Dialogue
Is Finally Closed

THE POLITICAL SITUATION

'There is only one person who is oppressed in this country. He is black. We are going to be reeling with strikes throughout the land and the Soweto uprisings are bound to be the order of the day, because our struggle here has been reduced by the white man, by his choice, to black versus white.'

Talking of 'change' in this country: I was in prison for the first time in 1958, my first pregnancy was there. And I was visited by my children in that same prison eighteen years later in 1976 – the very daughter that I had been expecting when I was in that prison the first time, in pursuit of the very same ideals!

When I looked at her, standing where her father had stood when he visited me there to prepare my defence twenty years earlier – nothing could have driven home this particular political lesson more clearly: I had moved nowhere politically from that stand in 1958. In 1976 I was still fighting the same battle; the political situation had not moved an inch from that day when I first entered that prison. When a daughter of mine visits me eighteen years thereafter and I stand there as a prisoner, worse off than I had been then, having been stripped much more of such rights as I had then (and the man who had stood there, her father, is serving a sentence of life in pursuit of the same ideals) – that tells you the kind of 'change' the government is talking about!

But the Afrikaners have become more vulnerable, in the sense that their own ideologies are falling apart. They are beginning to expose the falseness of each other's ideological beliefs. It is a trend nobody can reverse. *endurance The key, . .*

Some time back I received a letter from a young Afrikaner policeman, telling me he had terrible conflicts about the political situation in the country. He was involved in the Soweto uprising in 1976 and he wrote, 'You cannot imagine what it meant for a chap of my age to be subjected to a situation where you have to shoot fellow-children because their skin is of another colour. I can assure you, although I was given the instruction "Shoot to kill", I used to see to it that my gun faced the opposite direction. I did not fire a single shot.' He said his parents would never understand that, they would kill him if they knew. He pitched up one day – it was here in Brandfort – and visited me a few times. He came in his private car, parked down the road. When he disappeared – he was uneasy because he felt they were on his heels – he took the book about Nelson, *The Struggle is My Life*.

The fact that an Afrikaner youth, a policeman, talks like that to a black 'communist', Nelson's wife, shows you the extent of the division in Afrikanerdom.

I was asked by some students of the University of the Free State to give them papers on Black Consciousness. They wanted to know what's happening in the country, they wanted to know the black man's thinking in the eighties, and they asked me what they could do. They are discussing such questions. They have serious problems on the campuses.

There was an article in the Johannesburg *Sunday Express* on Hendrik van den Bergh.* Here was a man who sent a whole leadership to prison for life, turning round because he had quarrels with the regime and deciding to speak the truth at the end of the day, saying, Mandela was never a communist and he should never have been sentenced to life imprisonment after all. Van den Bergh was at the top! They knew the truth! Those who pass laws in Parliament and those who govern at the point of a bullet, they know the truth. They know that it is not a question of fighting communism, that their fight is against the black man. The so-called 'total onslaught' on the country, the so-called 'communist danger', is a frame-up. It is of no relevance to me personally what the

*Former head of BOSS (Bureau of State Security; now called the National Intelligence Service).

white man calls me in the pursuance of my political ideals. But they know. How else can they get the West to finance our oppression if they don't alarm the world with the so-called communist threat?

Of course, we also have conflicts within our movement. The South African situation is so complex that ideological differences cannot be avoided. The history of the African National Congress has been non-racialist; it took the form of various ethnic political groups working together in an interwoven structure and some people said that whites within the Congress Alliance were playing too prominent a role, but this was not the case. People had assumed positions on merit, because of their value politically. The question of colour did not matter. But then you get mischievous elements who insisted, together with the government, that the Congress of Democrats was just a shadow of the banned Communist Party, dominating all the other political organizations. The masses don't have funds, and the people who were able to raise funds internationally were white comrades.

The ANC is committed to non-racialism. The ANC cannot imagine a situation in which the white man does not exist. We never look at people as black or white; it is the enemy who compels us to use those terms. The umbrella organization of the ANC embodies everyone who is fighting side by side with us against oppression. The white student at Wits or Cape Town University who is beaten up by the same system that is beating up my people here in the Free State – must I ignore him? He is fighting the same cause as me. That is a fellow comrade. And you can't ignore those students who today are so brave as to hold anti-Republic demonstrations with a vacant chair labelled 'Nelson Mandela'. They are fellow human beings who are fighting side by side in our struggle. The South Africa of tomorrow that I'm fighting for will include that white child who has been so brave defying his Broederbond parents and shouting the slogans of my movement on the campus. I can't ignore him. He is part of us.

There are certain whites – Bram Fischer,* Helen Joseph, Gold-

---

*From a prominent Afrikaner family, a QC and a member of the Communist Party; one of the defence advocates in the Treason Trial, 1957–61; leading defence counsel in the Rivonia trial, 1963–4. In 1965, when on trial as a communist, he went underground to continue the struggle and was later sentenced to life imprisonment for participating in the same 'conspiracy' as the Rivonia defendants. He died of cancer in 1975. After the funeral, the prison authorities demanded that his ashes be returned to the jail.

berg,* Beyers Naudet† – you would never dream of thinking of them in terms of colour. Those whites, who are white in the law, are to us comrades and fellow freedom-fighters. I have as much respect for Helen Joseph as for my mother Lilian Ngoyi. I get a shock when I am reminded that they are white. They are part of us, of the cause, of our suffering. We are determined to create a harmonious racial situation in this country, including the white South African, the white student.

Now there is a school of thought in the Black Consciousness movement which wants to go it alone, excluding the white man. It is a misinterpretation of the political situation and can only be used by the system to divide the masses, who are now solidifying. It is irrelevant in the 1980s to discuss the ideological differences within a struggle that started four hundred years ago.

Steve Biko, for whom I have the greatest admiration and who was our national idol, is not so much the father of Black Consciousness as one of our greatest African Nationalists. That is what he understood himself to be, in the same way as we have African Nationalists on Robben Island. He merely expounded and exemplified ideologies that existed before. The ANC Youth League was founded back in the 1940s by the Sisulus, Mandelas and Mbekis for the same reason: the struggle needed to be Africanized, the militancy of the youth had to be emphasized and integrated. Today the racial laws are such that politically the races are forced to operate separately; that naturally gave impetus to the Black Consciousness movement. It was a historical necessity to conscientize the people. The white man had said: we will go it alone; and the black man's reaction was, we want to prove that we also can go it alone, that we don't need him. We are who we are; politically we are going to develop separately. And that's what's happened. There was a

---

*Dennis Goldberg, one of the accused in the Rivonia trial; sentenced to life imprisonment. After twenty-one years in Pretoria Prison he accepted a conditional release in March 1985.

†A prominent and internationally acclaimed critic of apartheid. Formerly a respected minister of the Dutch Reformed Church, he was ousted from his ministry because he stood by his conviction that the doctrine of apartheid was irreconcilable with the Gospel. He founded and directed the Christian Institute, a multiracial organization that worked towards reconciliation between the races. The CI was outlawed in 1977. Dr Naude was banned from 1977 to 1984. In February 1985 he was elected Secretary General of the South African Council of Churches in succession to Bishop Desmond Tutu, winner of the Nobel Peace Prize.

political vacuum – the banned ANC was forced to operate underground, whereas the Black Consciousness movement could operate openly. The leaders of the Black Consciousness movement knew the direction. They were and they are part and parcel of the struggle. They know who the enemy is: the government of this country.

The UDF, the United Democratic Front, is our South Africa of tomorrow, a movement that encompasses everybody, even people of different ideologies – the worker, the doctor, the lawyer, the man in the street, the road digger – that is our country. Those who sing Pretoria's tune against the UDF are doing so because they fear the people who are bringing about real change in this country. The UDF is a very serious threat to the government – they see it as a threat first raised by the ANC in the sixties. It is a common united front encompassing everybody, the biggest mass organization launched since then. That is why the government began arresting the leaders and organizers individually for this and that petty offence:* precisely what they did with the ANC before they banned it.

The government has cut our country up into enclaves. This enclave is for those Zulu Kaffirs, that enclave is for those Xhosa Kaffirs, that enclave is for those Pedi Kaffirs – that is what the so-called homeland puppets have accepted. Pretoria pulls the strings and directs them as to what they should think, and uses them to oppress their people. These people suck the dummies from their masters in Pretoria, where their feeding bottle is sterilized and refilled. They have become their master's voice. That's what they, in turn, are doing to our people in the so-called homelands.

The government thrives on deceiving the electorate. They want the white man to believe that the President's Council can be of relevance when these so-called constitutional reforms, which give so-called parliamentary representation to Indians and Coloured people, are just a monumental fraud, a propaganda exercise and a non-issue for blacks. It's not even worth discussing. Even if we had been included, it would have made no difference whatsoever. This is not what we are fighting for. We are fighting for the total liberation of the black man in this country. It is a national struggle we are fighting, not for a bunch of

*A series of arrests culminated in two treason trials of UDF leaders which opened in 1985.

stooges in a white-elephant parliament which always remains supreme. The black man does not want his chains changed into gold and polished. He does not even want copper chains. He is fighting for his total liberation and the total hacking off of those chains.

Our future South Africa will be multiracial. It will accommodate all of us. The wealth is enough for everybody. The Freedom Charter is a blueprint of our future government. Whatever adjustments have to be made will be made within that sacred document. It will be a socialist state – there is no other way of sorting out our starvation problems, the discrepancy between the population groups, the haves and the have-nots. Everyone will have a fair share of the wealth of this country.

As for the white parliamentary opposition, they can never unseat the Afrikaner nationalists who have been in power since 1948. They can never really propagate 'one man one vote', which is what we believe in, which is what we shall attain. And any man who is not fighting on that platform with us is of no relevance to the organization. One cannot dismiss the fact that such limited conscientization of the white minority as there is, is perhaps due to the PFP. It is up to them to continue to conscientize their people and get them to adjust to the inevitable black government of tomorrow.

The churches cannot play a direct political role. They can only identify with the struggle of the people, as they have been trying to do. They must involve themselves with the community, with politicizing the people. Some churches have joined us in the fight by taking up political issues – for instance, people like Bishop Tutu and the Anglican Church, the Roman Catholic Church, and the Methodists. For too long churches have confined themselves to religious affairs. The government has seen to it that they confine themselves to spiritual needs, when we have political needs. Our spirits are very rich. They don't need anybody's help. The introduction of Christianity to this country is identified by militants with the whole system of oppression: the white man came with a Bible in one hand and a gun in the other; he gave the black man the Bible while taking his land. He taught the black man that when master hits the one cheek, you turn the other. And while the white man was enjoying this heaven on this earth, he wanted us to believe we would have our share of the fat of the land in the next world. We don't want any spiritual fat of our land. But we want this wealth of this land we have built and we have sacrificed for.

For generations the attitude of the blacks towards religion has been one of devout submission. With the escalation of black theology, young men in the churches have tried to interpret religion correctly and to relate it to the present condition of the black man and his struggle. The churches are part of the oppressed masses of the country; the churches are the people. So they have a major role to play.

Nothing is more important than what is happening in the labour movement. We are the wealth of this country. We dig the wealth of this land. We could bring this country down through our labour – these black hands. We have made it what it is and we can bring it down in the same way. The people are there in industry – starving. They are there in the mines – starving. They are there as domestic servants – starving. It is not a question of outside agitators or communists from Russia. It is us, the people. We don't have to be told we are hungry. We *are* hungry. The government thinks it can divide us – separate the trade unions from the man in the township, when in fact the trade union is made up of the same people – the worker is the same man who leaves Soweto at one in the morning to be at the white man's factory at five, because the trains are choc-a-bloc. The worker is the same man who has been removed physically from his roots, from his father's land, a so-called 'black spot', and has been placed by a white man in an arid, uninhabitable place, a so-called 'homeland'; and this worker looks across and sees the graves of his children who have died of malnutrition in a land that is one of the richest in the world.

There is only one person who is oppressed in this country. He is black. We are going to be reeling with strikes throughout the land and the Soweto uprisings are bound to be the order of the day, because our struggle here has been reduced by the white man, by his choice, to black versus white.

No code of conduct will mean anything to the black worker – it is irrelevant.

The multinational companies, as far as we are concerned, are political criminals in this country. We wouldn't be where we are today – politically – if it hadn't been for these foreign companies. The role they are playing is simply to defuse a militant situation. If you give a man a salary comparable to that of his white counterpart, and he goes back to the ghetto where he has no rights and remains a 'Bantu' and must carry that document of oppression, that *dompass*,* you are only defusing and demoralizing him into believing that his situation is normal, because you claim that his work situation is normal. But that's not true, and it can never be.

That is why the foreign companies must get out. We are only interested in sanctions now. Every alternative has been examined by those men who have spent their lifetimes in prison. One doesn't dream for one minute that sanctions alone would bring the government down, or disinvestment alone. But it is part of a tool one can use. And in fact, tools of this nature which are instruments of liberation would lessen the bloodbath we are heading for, because you would expedite this long, long process of relieving the black man of his suffering. We know that foreign companies have literally financed our oppression; we know who our friends have been in the struggle.

It is not us, but the white man, who should be thinking of how he will fit into our future society. It's his problem. He has the audacity to talk about the protection of minority groups when he is oppressing the majority. The arrogance! That he sits there in power for over four hundred years, legislating against millions and millions of people and oppressing us for all these generations, and now we must worry about the protection of minority rights, and of his property and his culture.

We are interested in the preservation of human rights and human dignity, so we will continue reshaping our history of tomorrow. Politically, people's emotions have reached boiling point. The atmosphere is so explosive, you can actually feel the anger of the people.

It was never the policy of the ANC to be violent. All that this people's organization is doing is responding to the violence of the system. Our great leader, Chief Lutuli, said, 'When a man attacks my kraal, I must take my spear and defend my family' – a man who was one of the greatest Christians, who wouldn't have lifted up a stone to kill a fly. It was out of that context that Umkhonto we Sizwe was born. A non-violent organization was forced to take up the spear and defend the honour of the black man against an enemy which had been waging war since the arrival of Jan van Riebeek in 1652. We are determined to fight to the bitter end for the liberation of our people. I am afraid that the white regime will have to decide whether to give in, when they

Verdomdepass: literally, a 'damned pass'.

125

realize they are fighting a futile battle. It is their decision whether they want to give in violently or sensibly and save our country.

Terrorism was in fact introduced by the white man in this land in 1652. We used our spears and shields. We, the indigenous races of this country, lived harmoniously. The first acts of terrorism were when they shot our grandfathers and grabbed their land.

The white man has raped the black man's culture and used it as a machine to oppress him. That's where the role of the white missionary has been unforgivable. To say that that culture, which in fact meant respecting your elders, was atheism, that your belief in your ancestors, your respect for your grandfathers, was atheist and ungodly, that was where things went wrong. He told me that what I venerate most was backward and barbaric, referring to our grandfathers, our great warriors, our generals – to Chaka, to Makana and all those – as barbarians! Because in order to destroy me as a proud human being with that black dignity, he had to destroy my identity from the core of my culture.

Before I went into solitary confinement, I must tell you the truth, I made pronouncements on platforms and said things I hadn't tested myself on. I was a social worker, I was a mother; I knew that even though I was in a violent situation, if I was myself given a gun and told to go into a battlefield and shoot, I knew I wouldn't be able to do it. Deep down in my heart I was a social worker and that instinct to preserve human life was there, not only from a professional point of view – it was the centre of my person.

What happened during my detention was quite extraordinary. Now if the man I'm dealing with appeared carrying a gun – in defence of my principles I know I would fire. That is what they have taught me. I could never have achieved that alone.

You learn to test the quality of your ideals when they do those things to you year in and year out, they actually make a politician out of you. So the measures they impose on us really build us. I cannot pretend that today I wouldn't gladly go and water that tree of liberation with my own blood, if it means that the children I am bringing up under these conditions will not lead my kind of life. I do not want anyone else to lead it. I would love to think that I belong to the last generation that will experience what we have gone through.

That is the bitterness they create in us. You want to put a stop to it. And if need be, you will use their own methods, because that is the language they understand. The wall the Afrikaner erects around himself no one can penetrate, because he knows that in order to penetrate it himself he uses a gun. He knows, when you retaliate in the same way, that you are really talking to him. And that is what they are making of each and every black man.

At the moment it's irrelevant who helps the black man to get rid of the shackles of oppression. There is yet that extremely difficult transition period which will be more difficult than in any other country. It will be our own Vietnam. Our suffering of today is absolutely nothing. We are facing a very, very grim future.

When I was a child, I thought then we owned all. The freedom you have as a child, those undulating plains, beautiful greenery – how we would run from one end of the river to the other, running over rolling beautiful green hills.* I thought that was my country, that I had every reason to believe that was my fatherland, belonging to my father's parents. Then comes the grim realization when you grow up and a white man tells you that your own country doesn't belong to you and that you must have a piece of paper to stay there.

Our fight is simply the fight for our fatherland, dating back to the frontier war started by the British settlers. That's why I wouldn't dream for a second of leaving this country. To me it is an admission on my part that a thief who has come and stolen my land has got such powers over me that he can drive me out through the back door. I will never leave South Africa.

In the present political structure there is no room for dialogue any more. Not at all. That chapter was closed by the government on 12 June 1964, when they jailed the leadership. Dialogue can only take place on the release of all our leaders in prison, all the banned people and the return of all our exiled leaders. That's the only way one can shape the country's future. Anything else is a sheer waste of time. And even then it is questionable whether they would still be prepared for the dialogue they were prepared for twenty years ago. Can you spend a quarter of your life in prison and still be prepared for the dialogue with your jailers that you called for twenty years ago, before they locked

*Mrs Mandela was talking about the Transkei. The irony is that the government has told her she could leave South Africa to live there, in that so-called 'independent homeland'. 'Imagine the audacity of it!' she said. 'If anybody should leave South Africa, it's not me, it's the settler government.'

you up? The leadership would have to be involved in an entirely new kind of political thinking; perhaps a completely new basis for dialogue and negotiation.

Part of My Soul Went with Him

VISITS TO ROBBEN ISLAND AND POLLSMOOR

*'Going there is a fantastic feeling, it's like recharging your
batteries. I think it's because they give us so much inspiration, so
much courage. Of course they will come back to play their rightful
role in a black-ruled South Africa – and Nelson will be our Prime
Minister.'*

*In June 1964 Nelson Mandela and the other Rivonia men, Walter Sisulu,
Govan Mbeki, Ahmed Kathrada, Raymond Mhlaba, Elias Motsoaledi
and Andrew Mlangeni, arrived on Robben Island and began to serve their
life sentences. A flat, rocky, wind-swept outcrop of land surrounded by
turbulent seas, it lies some seven miles to the north-west of Cape Town. It
was mid-winter, dankly cold; on days of dense mist the foghorn from the
island's lighthouse echoed mournfully.*

*Mandela's cell in a new maximum-security 'isolation' section of eighty-
eight cells, separated from other blocks by a thirty-foot wall, was typical:
about seven feet square and lit by one bulb. Some thirty-three leaders and
'intellectuals' were in this section, while hundreds of other political prisoners
were confined in communal cells in the main blocks.*

*For the first ten years Mandela and his comrades laboured in a lime
quarry – a huge hole dug by generations of prisoners – under glaring summer
sun or in chill winter mists. Their diet consisted mainly of maize porridge and
stale vegetables. Psychological persecution and frequent physical assaults
accompanied the hard labour, which was later varied to include road repair
work and the collection of seaweed from beaches. One half-hour visit, one
letter, every six months; only personal and family matters could be discussed.*

Through hunger-strikes and go-slow protests, through international pressure and the continuing demands for improvements from Helen Suzman, the lone Progressive MP, and from the International Red Cross, reforms were gradually achieved: hard labour was ended; newspapers – hitherto forbidden – were permitted, and visits and letters were increased to two a month. Study meant more than any other 'privilege' – Mandela had begun by studying for a London law degree until post-graduate studies were banned, as was law as a subject for political prisoners. Since neither French nor German was allowed, he studied Afrikaans as well as economics and history.

In the special section there was a large yard – the men spent most of their time out of doors; they had exercise and sports.

Mac Maharaj, a fellow prisoner on Robben Island, said that Mandela had the confidence of all prisoners, whatever their political persuasion, and was accepted as their spokesman: 'He often guided us in the campaigns . . . and showed tremendous persistence. We have waged hunger strikes, we have waged go-slows. We have petitioned, filed written complaints and verbal complaints . . .

'I do not recall a time when he showed any despondence . . . not even when Winnie was in jail, detained or when news came out of her torture . . . has Nelson flagged. His confidence in the future has been growing.'

MEETINGS ON ROBBEN ISLAND

Dr Nthatho Motlana, the family doctor and guardian of the children, remembers a conversation with Nelson Mandela on Robben Island in 1976:

Oh powerful, powerful! Except for a few grey hairs he was the same Nel I have known for many years. Absolute dignity, a grand Xhosa chief! Extremely fit, mentally and physically. But our talk was interrupted every other minute – 'You stop talking about that thing or you're getting out now. I give you five minutes.' Even boxing was not allowed, and he was a boxer himself! Only family matters, for one hour.

Priscilla Jana, who used to be one of the family lawyers, saw Nelson Mandela for a consultation in 1977:

We brought an application for Zindzi. After Winnie was banished to

Brandfort, she was being very unduly harassed by the Security Police, and Zindzi was affected by all this, because Zindzi's friends could not come to the house. And according to South African law, once a woman is married she is regarded as a minor, which means she can't do proceedings or anything of her own accord. So in fact Winnie couldn't bring this application for Zindzi, who was a minor at that stage. Therefore we had to get the documents signed by Nelson.

It was a very memorable meeting. He hasn't been acting as a lawyer for fifteen years, but I must tell you, he commented on the documents as a lawyer, which was amazing, without letting emotionalism have an effect on him whatsoever. And we had a little incident. We took some food and wanted to have lunch with him during consultation. So we asked the officials whether we could give him the sandwiches, and they said no. So Nelson said, 'Oh, don't worry about it. Everything on this island depends on the whims and fancies of these officials.' So the prosecutor said, 'Well, Mr Mandela, it is prison regulations.' And Nelson said, 'I'm not even prepared to debate this issue with you!' After so many years he still commands that authority. He's got every quality of a statesman.

He's still very good-looking, he's got tremendous stature, he's got a fantastic physique. During our entire conversation he didn't complain about prison, he just wasn't interested in himself. I would have normally thought that when people are in prison what you are concerned about is your immediate home, how is my wife and my children, but his first question was: how are my people – and he went on very philosophically – tell them that there was still hope and it's not going to be long and they must know that he still is with them. The way he incorporated it in our discussion, the warders were not quick enough to catch on with that.

Suddenly, in April 1982, Mandela, Sisulu, Kathrada, Mhlaba and Mlangeni were transferred from the island to Pollsmoor Maximum Security Prison on the mainland, some miles from Cape Town.

A year later, during a visit, Mandela managed to convey to his wife information about conditions in this new prison: nothing dramatic, essentially the fact that men who had struggled for nearly twenty years to achieve improvements now found a great deterioration: for instance, whereas on the island each man had a cell, in Pollsmoor six of them – the sixth a young newcomer – were together in one large cell; whereas on the island they had moved freely in the communal atmosphere of their section, now they were isolated from all other prisoners. There were no walks as on the island; they had an exercise yard attached to the cell from which they could only see the sky. Mandela now understood what Oscar Wilde had meant by 'the little patch of blue that prisoners call the sky'.

During the 1970s and 1980s, a Free Mandela Campaign initiated in South Africa attracted worldwide support. Mandela had come to symbolize all political prisoners in South Africa. By 1985 the British and American governments had joined in pressing for his release.

I never had a reference book all these years; I couldn't be registered in any job, that's another reason why I lost so many jobs. And in 1965 they said: 'You have applied to see your husband? You won't see him without a pass.' They came and picked me up from home and took me to the pass office; they filled out the forms themselves. So that's how I came to get it.

I have to apply to the local magistrate for a permit to leave the district each time I visit Nelson. I am barred from using trains and I am not allowed to use the car to get there, so I have to fly at tremendous cost. A lot of friends have spent a fortune on my trips.

The permit prescribes that I must take the shortest route from the airport to Caledon Square, the police station where I report my arrival, and from there take the shortest route to my friends'. house in Elsie's River. There I remain confined to the house. I cannot even go outside the gate. From the time I arrive I find police cars waiting, parked outside the house right through twenty-four hours. They actually take shifts. When Nelson was on Robben Island I had to go from that house direct to the embarkation office, where I joined the queue of visitors from all over the country, coming directly from the trains.

I had to sign the same book I had been signing for the last twenty years. You are not allowed to bring cameras, no cats, no dogs, no children under sixteen, and already, there, you are warned to limit your conversation to family affairs. The permit for the journey is 50c. Then you walk ten steps down to the quay where you enter a little boat. Sometimes when the sea is rough, they just cancel the trip – you are at the mercy of these officers. That means all the visitors have taken the long journey to Cape Town in vain. The journey to the island takes forty-five minutes. In the past they used to put a special chair for me in a special corner of the boat. Of course I ignored that. Really, to be confined in a prison ferry on a chair was lunatic. So I just sat where everybody else was sitting.

When you arrive at the island you are met by prison officials who accompany you. On the left is a high grey stone wall which shuts the island off and on the right is the open sea.

You walk straight to a big door; the entrance to the waiting-room, which has a few chairs. I remember a big shell ashtray on the windowsill, always full of cigarette butts, and I always wondered who was there before me. The two toilets were always filthy. Three officers would parade up and down while one stood at the door, making you feel you were part of the prison population. The whole atmosphere was cold and brutal.

Then some senior officer calls out your name: 'Mrs Mandela, you can come now.' But before that he reminds you each time – I must be extremely dumb – for nearly twenty years: 'By the way, you must talk about your family and the children and that's all. Nothing political; if we feel there is something we don't understand in your conversation, we shall cut your visit.'

Sometimes they put additional restrictions on our conversation: for instance, when one of our children was arrested and when there were attempts on my life, which were mentioned in the local press, or when heads of state from all over the world had sent telegrams for Nelson's birthday to my address – all this was not allowed.

I was always called in last to a little room at the end of a passage.

There were three warders behind me and three behind him. The lighting was very bad and the glass partition so thick – I could never see a clear picture of him, just a silhouette really. I think he has a better view of me. He jocularly used to say I must stand back so that he could see what I was wearing. We had to talk through earphones which they could switch off any time. And of course we were once again reminded not to talk about anything but the family. If, for instance, I mentioned a name they didn't know – grandchildren, we call them by all kinds of names – they disconnected the phone and politely asked me what we were talking about. It used to be very bad. Visits were stopped altogether on some occasions. We used to have violent exchanges with the officers; he would address them as the boys they are.

When you have been a prisoner as long as I have, there is a certain communicating language just known between the two of you. I think that's the case with every one of us. This develops on its own, so you are able to convey quite a lot.

The warders have come to treat him very respectfully. His attitude is somehow as if they are his Praetorian guard. He has maintained his role within prison itself; he has continued looking after his family of black people even in there. He does so much welfare work, exactly as he did outside.

On the island he used to spend half the time discussing family problems of the prisoners. I gathered that he'd got special permission throughout the years to do that because they were not part of the family. Some of the prisoners who had been there for, say, ten years, without having had any contacts with their families, he would give me instructions about them. We have a lot of broken homes in our society, children who land up in prison, and he would ask me to raise funds for their education which he would channel to them.

I would sit there like a little girl. I sometimes think, for him I am a continuation of his children. He cannot imagine that I've grown up. When he wants me to do something, sometimes I feel like saying: don't you think that this is a bit difficult? But then he says it again, he repeats it a bit slower, and you just can't say no.

Zindzi is the only one who dares to interrupt him occasionally, if she feels he is not right or that he is demanding too much. But it usually ends up the same way. 'Darling,' he would say gently, 'just think about it again,' and she would go and do it. When Nelson asks you to do something, you do it. Arguing you can start later. He is not authoritative as such, but he communicates with you in such a way that you can't question what he says. For instance, when there was something important I wanted to tell him, I'd rehearse it before I would talk to him. (*Laughs.*) Sometimes I would even write it down to hear how it sounds.

After forty-five minutes they would say: 'Time is up!' We kissed farewell through the glass partition.

Except for the little I can gather from his letters, I have no idea what Nelson does with himself through the day. When his study facilities were withdrawn for four years, that was really bad. He was supposed to have abused his study facilities. He told me that they claimed to have found memoirs he was supposed to have written somewhere in prison.

He had asked them to bring those memoirs to him. After a year he was still waiting for them. I don't know what actually happened.

So I sent him the *Reader's Digest* guide-book of South Africa – it is really meant for tourists. It was sent back. I sent him *The Boer War* – surely that should show him how strong the powers he was trying to fight are; that's the type of thing that should deflate his spirit, if anything, and the prison authorities would be happy for him to see the might of this land. It was sent back.

Until recently even gifts of food were returned. What harm would it have done if you'd sent a box of chocolates to a man doing life imprisonment! We weren't allowed to give him a watch for his birthday. He can only see and touch the presents before they are taken away. The only thing that is allowed is money.

There have always been speculations about his health. In 1981 Harry Pitman – a white politician! – said publicly that Nelson had cancer. I don't know where he got it from and why he said such a cruel thing and why he thought he was the Mandela family spokesman. Supposing it had been true, it would have been the responsibility of the family to release that to the public. It's this master–servant relationship, they think they know everything better about us! So to counter this silly claim by Harry Pitman, the authorities brought me all the medical files on Nelson from the day he entered prison. It was such a wonderful feeling to see all these little things he had suffered from, the colds, how he had Disprins prescribed – I told you he doesn't believe in tablets, he believes in exercise! The last entry was a conversation between him and a senior physician, in which he said that he was worried about his weight, from 77 kg it was now 80. The doctor prescribed a high-protein diet. So now he has fish for supper. It was the first time I heard what my husband eats, from prison records!

All he lives for – besides of course the knowledge that he'll come out one day – is the letters and family visits that have played an extremely important role in his life, and one of the things he enjoys most is visits from his children. (Children's visits are prohibited from the age of two up to sixteen.) He didn't bring them up, they had to be introduced to him – one of the most traumatic experiences for all of us. It is not easy for a mother to say: 'Look, your father, he is doing life in prison.' It is not easy for a child to go and see that father she has heard so much about in those conditions, in that atmosphere. Psychologically, it's a fifty-fifty sort of thing. You never know what the child's reaction is going to be: either break-down or the child emerges solid as a rock from the experience, and proud of seeing father.

Because, how do you bring up a child in this kind of society – you can't have any sense of crime in this country if you have brought up a child to be proud of parents behind bars. In a child's mind a criminal is in fact somebody who fights for liberation – how can you teach children otherwise?

Zindzi recalls her first visit to her father after she had turned sixteen:

'I was a bit apprehensive, I thought, Jesus, this is meant to be my father. What am I going to say? Will he be proud of me? Have I lived up to his standards? But he is such a warm person, and he is so tactful. He said: "Oh, darling, I can see you now as a kid at home on my lap" – and I immediately forgot the surroundings, and we started dreaming and dreaming and then I felt so free; and he has this terrific sense of humour, so it went on so well.

'My father is still so much in touch, he knows what's happening. For instance he says to me: "Darling, I hope you won't be paying the increased rents. You mustn't do that." Or when newspapers are boycotted, he says that I mustn't buy them. He managed to get that across.

'They really respect my father. One of the warders even took his grandchild for a walk during a visit. These people can be humane when they feel like it.

'We were always called in last. We see the other prisoners going out and when they pass, we see them giving the thumbs-up sign. They still look so young, so dignified.

'The spirit of those political prisoners, when you meet the ex-islanders, is so strong. There is so much unity there, and outside there are so many divisions. The same spirit as in the fifties, it hasn't faded. And someone was telling me that Walter Sisulu is considered the confidant – everybody confides in Sisulu when they have a problem; Govan Mbeki is the philosopher; and Mandela is considered the father, the leader.'

Had Nelson not been what he is, he could have been one of the greatest psychologists. He is able to read people's personalities from almost nothing, just from the handwriting. He would tell me, for instance, when you wrote that mistake, when you scratched out that word, you must have been doing this and that, and it will be dead accurate! A mind doesn't make a mistake, just like that. There is a reason. And you have to tell him your state of mind when you made that mistake, so that he could analyse that in order that you don't make that mistake again.

He is a complete lawyer through and through. He is a perfectionist without imposing himself. He philosophizes a great deal. This is his natural self. I hardly lived with him. So I only discovered that side of his life when he was on the island. Zindzi has inherited a great deal of that disposition. He could also have been a writer if he had had the opportunity.

EXTRACTS FROM LETTERS FROM NELSON MANDELA ON ROBBEN ISLAND TO WINNIE MANDELA

6 May 1979

I had hoped to discuss with Zindzi the project* you said she would undertake this yr. My considered view, subject to what she may say, is that she must keep out certain characters from her work. Naturally such works must give a faithful account of the events, the pleasant and unpleasant. The personalities mentioned, even those that are very dear to her, must appear not as angels, but as real men of flesh and blood with virtues and weaknesses.

Recently autobiographies that are frighteningly frank and sensational, especially from the younger generation, are coming out. Some go so far as to discuss such intimate matters and border on something many would regard as positively improper. Have you seen the books of Sophia Loren and Margaret Trudeau, ex-wife of the Candian Premier? I am not in a position to judge to what extent the latter's book has damaged the political career of Premier Trudeau. A happy family life is an important pillar to any public man. All the same, Zindzi's work would serve wider issues and its main aim would not be the commercial one or desire for publicity.

Had it not been for your visits, wonderful letters and your love I would have fallen apart many yrs ago. I paused here and drank some coffee, after which I dusted the photos on my bookcase. I start with that of Zeni, which is on the outer side, then Zindzi's and lastly yours, my darling Mum. Doing so always eases the longing for you.

*A family biography.

2 September 1979

You will be quite right to regard '79 as women's year.* They seem to be demanding that society should live up to its sermons on sex equality. The French lady, Simone Veil, has lived through frightful experiences to become President of the European Parliament, while Maria Pintassilgo cracks the whip in Portugal. From reports it is not clear who leads the Carter family. There are times when Carter's Rosalyn seems to be wearing the trousers. I need hardly mention the name of Margaret Thatcher! Despite the collapse of her worldwide empire and her emergence from the Second World War as a third-rate power, Britain is in many respects still the centre of the world. What happens there attracts attention from far and wide. Indira will rightly remind us that in this respect Europe is merely following the example of Asia, which in the last two decades has produced no less than two lady premiers. Indeed she may have added that past centuries have seen many female rulers: Isabella of Spain, Elizabeth I of England, Catherine the Great of Russia (how great she really was I don't know), the Batokwa Queen, Mantatisi and many more. But all these became first ladies in spite of themselves – through heredity. Today the spotlight falls on those women who have pulled themselves up by their own bootstraps. For these '79 has yielded quite a harvest . . .

On 16 August I saw an orthopaedic surgeon and he examined my right heel which worries me now and again. I will discuss the matter further with Dr Edelstein on his next round to the island. That morning the *Dias* carried me to Cape Town the sea was rough and though I occupied a sheltered spot on the deck, it seemed that rain was falling. The boat rocked on endlessly taking every wave on its prows. Midway between the island and Cape Town an army of demons seemed to be on the rampage and, as the *Dias* was tossed about, it looked as if a thousand irons were falling apart. I kept my eyes glued on a lifebelt a few paces away. There were about five officials in between me and the belt, two young enough to be my grandsons. I said to myself, 'If something happens and this boat goes under, I will commit my last sin on earth and tender my humble apologies when I reach heaven. I will run over them all and be the first on that belt.' Fortunately no disaster overtook us.

*Political prisoners were still not permitted to discuss prison conditions or events in South Africa, but certain limited references to foreign affairs were allowed.

But about you, darling Mum, what can I tell you? At forty-five you have changed so much from the night we sat alone in the open veld south of the city. Yet as the youth drains away from your veins, as your once full and smooth face shows signs of erosion and the magnetic complexion that made you so desirable in the '50s continues to fade, the more you become adorable, the more I long to cuddle up to you. You are everything a mum should be. Happy Birthday, darling Mum! I LOVE you!!

Devotedly, Madiba.

1.3.81

I wish you the best of luck in the exams and in the pending case.* Your good academic record allows me to hope that you will make it, even though you have doubts about the outcome. I regard your doubts as no more than the modesty of one who wants to be absolutely certain before she can make predictions. Again, my very best wishes.

As far as the case is concerned we will need much more than good luck; so much will be at stake for all those involved. This court has always made every one of your cases, however trivial the actual charge may be, something more than an ordinary court trial, in which luck hardly played a role in your discharge. Only the determination, loyalty and skill of professional friends pulled you out. I am confident that, whatever the final verdict may be, they will again do their best.

Although I always try to put up a brave face, I never get used to you being in the cooler. Few things disorganize my whole life as much as this particular type of hardship, which seems destined to stalk us for quite some time still. I will never forget the desperately distressing experiences we had from May '69 to September '70 and the six months you spent in Kroonstad.

To ask someone to live with you (if you did) was a necessary precaution on your part and was by no means intended to be an act of defiance against anyone. It is a perfectly reasonable action which ought to raise no alarm. I expect you to inform me of the date of the hearing and the final outcome. Meanwhile I will be thinking of you, especially as you are ordered to the dock, and as you listen to the expected and unexpected turns in the state evidence. I am solidly behind you and know too well that you suffer because of your love

*Winnie Mandela was accused of violating her banning order by having a lodger in her house in Brandfort. The case had been postponed from May 1980.

of and loyalty to the children and me as well as to our large family. It is an ever-growing love and loyalty, which take me more forcefully every time you come.

I do no longer remember whether the young fellow involved is still Mokgoro whom you once sent to school in Orlando West. In what class is he? Is there a high school now in Phathakahle? I am confident that from the point of view of his personal welfare, he will benefit a lot from his succession with you, and that you will try within your own means to look after him well. I would have liked to surprise him with a postcard or short letter. But I don't even want to try, because none would go through. But do give him my warmest regards . . .

I naturally assume that you have already congratulated Tembi* and fiancé on their engagement and that you will soon send them a present. Perhaps an auto- or biography of some prominent woman, say, Olive Schreiner, would be just the thing she would love. The book could be signed by you, Zeni and Zindzi and carefully selected friends like Granny . . .

I am sending the books in four separate boxes to Zindzi in Orlando and I hope that you will be able to see them. Most of them are Afrikaans books, but there are others, including one by the famous psychologist, Carl Jung. You might like to read that.

I am writing to Ismail to thank him for the many things he has done for us . . . I hope you will work together with Zindzi, Ismail and George† in drafting the letter to those who kindly sponsored our candidature for the Chancellorship of the University of London. The support of 7,199 against such prominent candidates‡ must have inspired the children and all our friends inside and outside the country. To you in particular it must have been even more inspiring, turning that miserable shack into a castle, making its narrow rooms as spacious as those of Windsor. I want all our supporters to know that I did not expect to poll even 100, to say nothing of 7,199, against a British princess and against so distinguished an English reformer as Mr Jack Jones. That figure has a significance far more than can be expressed in a note written under my current circumstances . . .

You have lost a bit of weight and I am not the only one who thinks so. Nonetheless you looked well and highly seductive, especially on

*Oliver and Adelaide Tambo's daughter.
†Ismail Ayob and George Bizos, lawyers who have represented the Mandela family for many years.
‡Princess Anne was elected.

Sunday morning with your earrings hanging down to your breasts!
I wanted to kiss the glass partition at the end of the visit.

When my husband was transferred to Pollsmoor Prison in Cape
Town in April 1982, the most logical explanation in the public mind
was that they wanted to bring him closer to Groote Schuur hospital –
there must be some truth in those rumours after all. It was a shocking
thing for all of us. The inquiries that came were just unbearable.

I didn't know about it. I was studying at home one day and just sent
one of the children to get me the newspaper and there I see the front-
page story and I also heard it from television in the evening. Some time
later I got a letter from the Prison Department – in the usual cold way –
informing me that my husband had been transferred to Pollsmoor
Prison.

My first trip there was an unforgettable experience. The drive to the
prison itself through the plushest suburbs of Cape Town, the most
beautiful scenery with those original colonial buildings – an area I had
never been to because I get confined to the address I usually stay at
down there. I just prayed that he had also seen that scenery, the
vineyards, the beauty of this country he was dying for. Because having
been confined to the island for twenty years, obviously he had forgotten
about the ordinary vegetation, how lovely the country is.

When we arrived we saw this handsome structure; it doesn't look
like a prison but like one of those modern technical institutions – a huge
complex, more than 6,000 prisoners. From the gates, of course, you
realize that you are in a maximum-security prison; heavily armed guards
at the entrance, the usual thing. Then we were ushered into a sitting-
room to wait for the visit – a completely different scene from Robben
Island.

In the section for visits, the glass partition was such that at least you
could see him as far as his waist. They have boxes that transmit the
sound, not the phone system any more. The voice gets amplified and
his voice came out much clearer.

He looked very, very well. The first question, of course, was why he
had been transferred. He had no idea. The most logical reason seems
to have been that it was for administrative reasons. He told me that the
very day he was transferred, he had been consulting a lawyer from Cape
Town about the education of young prisoners on the island. He had

just received a cheque of about R14,000 for their studies. Many of them had been imprisoned after the uprising in 1976; he had been able to help them continue with their studies.

The Prisons Department must have got worried about the extent to which he was doing this sort of programme. The island became known as Mandela University. Youths who had left school having Standard 6 emerged from the island with degrees. In his absence that programme came to an end.

Incidentally, he hadn't seen one tree on his way to that prison. They were transported in an army truck which could take ten elephants and they were put in some special cage, he said. There were three of them; they had to stand all the way. It is about an hour's drive to the prison.

He said the last time he saw a blade of grass was on the island, as he was leaving. Now he can only see the sky. The prison is in a valley. He must be in a part of the prison that is so enclosed that he can't even have the view of the mountains. Isn't it strange that there can still be a difference between nothing and nothing? That island – which was nothing, which was death itself – suddenly became a paradise. There he had a cell with his name engraved on the door to give him that psychological feeling of eternity, of a total end – this is the end of life. There he had that little garden where he used to till the land with a fork and watch plants grow and he was free to move around in the big yard. The irony of it all! Pollsmoor is a virtual palace when you compare the structure itself to the island. Yet he is certainly worse off there than he was on the island.

He and Uncle Walter and the other four who are confined together – in a cold, damp cell with no privacy for themselves or for their studies – are isolated from all other prisoners. That is soul-killing. In fact, they are subjecting him now to more harassment of the soul than he ever had on the island. Those colleagues there were a community he adjusted to for twenty years. To deprive him even of that! What kind of fear drives people to this type of insanity!

Officer Gregory, who came with them from the island, was very pleasant. For instance, on our arrival he might say, 'Your husband will come down just now, he is still showering and shaving. He must look very nice for you. I hope you won't mind the delay of a few minutes.' I never got that kind of conversation on the island. There they said at the end of a visit: 'Time is up!' Here, Gregory would say: 'Mrs Mandela, you still have five minutes.'

Nelson is that same man who left us those many years ago and who will come back to us in that same spirit. Nelson exudes that. You don't have to ask, you don't have to be told, if you know him as we do. His spirit remains untouched. All those men are just as untouched as he is. They are absolutely fantastic. Such total dedication, such total commitment, no soul erosion whatsoever; they are all like that. They are totally liberated, of course. It is a government in exile. The fact that they are incarcerated is just a reality they have to put up with. It is the mutual inspiration they give each other and the unshakeable belief that they are fighting for a just cause; and the incoming new prisoners support them in the knowledge that the struggle outside continues.

Nelson commands the same authority he's always commanded without exerting himself. It is there, you just can't ignore it, nor can any police officer, be he black or white.

One day, when Zindzi and I were going to visit him on Robben Island, they had cancelled all the ferries because the sea was too rough. But Nelson insisted on our coming. He wanted to see us. They phoned from the island and we got tablets against seasickness and we went. Our boat was the only one that day. We were singing all the way and didn't even feel the rough seas.

Then, suddenly Zeni, her husband and baby daughter, Zamaswazi, were allowed contact visits – diplomatic treatment because she is married to a member of the royal family of Swaziland. Zeni said:

> 'He had never held a baby for sixteen years. He had seen us but never touched us. I thought he would break down. But I thought if I keep my strength, then Daddy won't. I went up to him, I nearly dropped the child, I couldn't believe we had a contact visit. I gave the child to my husband and just ran to my father, we must have held each other for a very long time. There were two policemen standing just behind my dad. Then he took the child and he held the baby all the time. He noticed that she needed her nappies changed and he even made her burp, like he just knew what to do. Then he played with her and she went to sleep.'

The following year when I took Zamaswazi along, it was very painful. She couldn't see Nelson properly on the other side of the barrier and she kept banging on the glass: 'Open, daddy! Open, daddy! I want to come in.' And Nelson smiled and said: 'Here are the keys darling', pointing to the warders. 'Ask them to open.' And she became more hysterical: 'Open, daddy, I want to sit on your lap!' Oh, that visit was terrible. I think I even saw tears in the eyes of the warders.

On the weekend of 12 to 13 May 1984, we had our first 'contact visit'. Can you imagine! We last touched his hand in 1962. When I arrived at Pollsmoor Prison – Zeni and her youngest were with me – Sergeant Gregory called me to the office. I got a terrible shock, I thought Nelson was sick, because that's very unusual. He said: 'As from now on you will be able to have different visits. I thought I should bring the news gently to you.' We kissed Nelson and held him a long time. It is an experience one just can't put into words. It was fantastic and hurting at the same time.

He clung to the child right through the visit.

Gregory, his warder, was so moved, he looked the other way. That the system could have been so cruel as to deny us that right for the last twenty-two years! Why deny that right to a man who is jailed for life?

I look forward to visits so much, but the trip back is awful – I feel so empty. I can't help thinking of all those years of our lives that are going down the drain – our best years.

Of course, what sustains you is the knowledge that one day they will come back to join us. You look forward to the next visit even as you come back. Going there is a fantastic feeling, it's like recharging your batteries. I think it's because they give us so much inspiration, so much courage. Of course they will come back to play their rightful role in a black-ruled South Africa.

The government has offered a few times to 'release' him on condition that he settles in 'his' homeland, the Transkei. Of course he has refused. To offer him that kind of 'freedom' after he has given twenty-two years of his life to the struggle! It's not even worth discussing. We would be back to square one. The latest release offer to Mandela in February '85 on condition that he renounces violence just proves the point.

The anger of the people cannot be contained any longer. The South African economy is almost bankrupt, and the international community is at last beginning to turn its back on South Africa economically because of its racial policy. What has happened now is that they have realized that the leaders of the people were correct after all, when they predicted this instability all those years ago in 1964. Their prediction that acts of violence would escalate, that polarization between the races would increase – that was the reading of history by sensitive men, men who had taken decisions, not lightly, to resort to the armed struggle.

This regime has built its own Frankenstein. How do they release that Frankenstein? The only solution is to release those men and do what they asked for years ago. But the Afrikaner nationalists cannot afford to lose face to the electorate.

The right wing and extreme right are at each other's throats. If only they had listened to the people's voice, the country wouldn't be faced with the political morass it is faced with today.

The problem is how to release these leaders in a South Africa that has not taken one step forward as far as the masses of this country are concerned – how do you release them to the same conditions they gave their lives to change?

Not one of the ideals contained in the Freedom Charter has been realized. How do you release men who gave up their lives for these ideals to exactly the same conditions, where they have to have these dehumanizing stamps in those dehumanizing passports to seek work – a book to determine where those men must live, where they should seek work? What freedom are they being offered? What freedom do you give to men who must still seek permission from the very same people who jailed them for these ideals? What freedom do you release them to when the races are still living as apart as ever and the situation is far worse than it was twenty-two years ago. What freedom are they being given when they are released to a country that is at each other's throats – all races fighting one another?

Botha is talking in terms of the freedom of the prisoners – totally different wavelengths! These men have at no stage gone to prison for *their* freedoms. These men went to prison for the freedom of the peace-loving people of this land. They gave up their lives for the freedom of the owners of this land, the black man. No prisoner in the whole world is consulted about his freedom. As Mandela has said, only free men negotiate.

On 31 January 1985, President P. W. Botha announced that the government would consider Nelson Mandela's release on condition that he gave a commitment that he would not 'make himself guilty of planning, instigating or committing acts of violence for the furtherance of political objectives'. The other Rivonia men serving life sentences received a similar 'offer'.

Nelson Mandela's reply was read on his behalf by his daughter Zindziswa in Jabulani Stadium in Soweto on 10 February 1985:

On Friday my mother and our attorney saw my father at Pollsmoor Prison to obtain his answer to Botha's offer of conditional release.

The prison authorities attempted to stop this statement being made but he would have none of this and made it clear that he would make the statement to you, the people.

[My father] should be here himself to tell you what he thinks of this statement by Botha. He is not allowed to do so. My mother, who also heard his words, is also not allowed to speak to you today.

My father and his comrades at Pollsmoor Prison send their greetings to you, the freedom-loving people of this, our tragic land, in the full confidence that you will carry on the struggle for freedom.

He, with his comrades at Pollsmoor Prison, sends his warmest greetings to Bishop Tutu, who has made it clear to the world that the Nobel Peace Prize belongs to you, who are the people. We salute him.

My father and his comrades at Pollsmoor Prison are grateful to the United Democratic Front, who without hesitation made this venue available to them so that they could speak to you today. My father and his comrades wish to make this statement to you, the people, first. They are clear that they are accountable to you and to you alone. And that you should hear their views directly and not through others.

My father speaks not only for himself and for his comrades at Pollsmoor Prison but he hopes he also speaks for all those in jail for their opposition to apartheid, for all those who are banished, for all those who are in exile, for all those who suffer under apartheid, for all those who are opponents of apartheid and for all those who are oppressed and exploited. Throughout our struggle there have been puppets who have claimed to speak for you. They have made this claim, both here and abroad. They are of no consequence. My father and his colleagues will not be like them.

My father says: 'I am a member of the African National Congress. I have always been a member of the African National Congress and I will remain a member of the African National Congress until the day I die. Oliver Tambo is much more than a brother to me. He is my greatest friend and comrade for nearly fifty years. If there is any one amongst you who cherishes my freedom, Oliver Tambo cherishes it more and I know that he would give his life to see me free. There is no difference between his views and mine.'

My father says: 'I am surprised at the conditions that the Government wants to impose on me. I am not a violent man. My colleagues and I wrote in 1952 to Malan asking for a round-table conference to find a solution to the problems of our country but that was ignored.

When Strijdom was in power, we made the same offer. Again it was ignored. When Verwoerd was in power we asked for a national convention for all the people in South Africa to decide on their future. This, too, was in vain.

It was only then when all other forms of resistance were no longer open to us that we turned to armed struggle.

Let Botha show that he is different to Malan, Strijdom and Verwoerd.

Let him renounce violence.

Let him say that he will dismantle apartheid.

Let him unban the people's organization, the African National Congress.

Let him free all who have been imprisoned, banished or exiled for their opposition to apartheid.

Let him guarantee free political activity so that the people may decide who will govern them.

I cherish my own freedom dearly but I care even more for your freedom. Too many have died since I went to prison. Too many have suffered for the love of freedom. I owe it to their widows, to their orphans, to their mothers and to their fathers who have grieved and wept for them. Not only I have suffered during these long, lonely, wasted years.

I am not less life-loving than you are. But I cannot sell my birthright, nor am I prepared to sell the birthright of the people to be free. I am in prison as the representative of the people and of your organization, the African National Congress, which was banned. What freedom am I being offered while the organization of the people remains banned? What freedom am I being offered when I may be arrested on a pass offence? What freedom am I being offered to live my life as a family with my dear wife who remains in banishment in Brandfort? What freedom am I being offered when I must ask for permission to live in an urban area?

What freedom am I being offered when I need a stamp in my pass to seek work? What freedom am I being offered when my very South African citizenship is not respected? Only free men can negotiate. Prisoners cannot enter into contracts. Herman Toivo Ja Toivo,* when freed, never gave any undertaking, nor was he called upon to do so.

I cannot and will not give any undertaking at a time when I and you the people are not free. Your freedom and mine cannot be separated. I will return.

EXCHANGE OF LETTERS BETWEEN NELSON MANDELA IN POLLSMOOR PRISON AND WINNIE MANDELA IN BRANDFORT

4.2.85

Zindzi's telegram reporting the death of Niki† shook me violently and I have not recovered yet from that shock. On occasions like this I often wonder just how far more difficult it would have been for me to take the decision to leave you behind if I had been able to see clearly the countless perils and hardships to which you would be exposed in my absence. I sincerely think that my decision would, nonetheless, have been easily the same, but it would certainly have been preceded by far more heart-searching and hesitation than was the case twenty-four years ago.

As I see it, the true significance of marriage lies not only in the mutual love which unites the parties concerned, although that is undoubtedly one of its cornerstones, but also in the faithful support which the parties guarantee – that it will always be there in full measure at critical moments.

Your love and support, the raw warmth of your body, the charming children you have given the family, the many friends you have won, the hope of enjoying that love and warmth again, is what life and happiness mean to me. I have somebody I love who is worthy to be loved and trusted, one whose own love and patient support have given me so much strength and hope.

Yet there have been moments when that love and happiness, that trust and hope, have turned into pure agony, when conscience and

*A leader of SWAPO, the South-West African People's Organization of Namibia.
†Winnie Mandela's sister.

148

a sense of guilt have ravaged every part of my being, when I have wondered whether any kind of commitment can ever be sufficient excuse for abandoning a young and inexperienced woman in a pitiless desert, literally throwing her into the hands of highwaymen; a wonderful woman without her pillar and support at times of need.

That agony tortures me when I consider that within the space of a relatively short time you have lost no less than four members of the family – CK, Nali, Lungile and now Niki. It is a grievous blow, very difficult to bear, and I wish I could be there, put you on my lap and remind you of all the good things with which your name is linked and help you to forget about the tragedies which have repeatedly overtaken the family . . .

Knowing full well just how you care for all people, especially the family, I am always extremely worried how you will react to each tragedy. That is what has worried me since Zindzi's telegram arrival, and that concern will not ease until I see you.

20.2.85

I returned in the early hours of today after almost three sad weeks of the most emotional storms in our life of separation. I however had one thing to look forward to, the letter from you which I knew would make my year. I knew it would reconstruct my shattered soul and restore it to my faith – the nation. Moments of such self-indulgence bring shame to me at such times when I think of those who have paid the supreme price for their ideological beliefs. Some of those fallen ones were dearer to me than my own life.

The letter was there, dated 4.2.85. I'm rereading it for the umpteenth time. Contrary to your speculation at first, I do not think I would have had the fibre to bear it all if you had been with me. You once said I should expect the inevitable fact that the struggle leaves debris behind; from that moment those many years ago I swore to my infinitesimal ego that I would never allow myself to be part of that political quagmire.

If life is comprised of the things you enumerate and hold dear, I am lost for words due to the fact that in my own small way life feels a little more monumental, material and demanding of one's innermost soul. That is why the love and warmth that exude from you behind those unkind concrete grey monotonous and cruel walls simply overwhelms me, especially when I think of those who in the name of the struggle have been deprived of that love.

149

You refer to moments when love and happiness, trust and hope have turned into pure agony, when conscience and sense of guilt have ravaged every part of your being. It is true, darling, I've lost so much of what is dearest to me in the years of our separation. When you have lived alone as I've done as a young bride and never known what married life is all about you cling to minute consolations, the sparing of one from the indignities that ravage us. In our case, with all those we have lost, the dignity of death has been respected ...

I was so proud of your message* to us. I've often wondered how I would have reacted if I had met you, Uncle Walter and others on the Pollsmoor steps and was told to take you home ...

*Mandela's reply to President Botha.

FREEDOM CHARTER

Drafted by a subcommittee of the National Action Council from contributions submitted by groups, individuals and meetings all over South Africa, approved by the ANC National Executive and adopted at the Congress of the People held at Kliptown near Johannesburg on 25–26 June 1955.

Each section of the charter was adopted by acclamation with a show of hands and shouts of 'Afrika'.

PREAMBLE

We, the people of South Africa, declare for all our country and the world to know:

That South Africa belongs to all who live in it, black and white, and that no government can justly claim authority unless it is based on the will of the people.

That our people have been robbed of their birthright to land, liberty and peace by a form of government founded on injustice and inequality;

That our country will never be prosperous or free until all our people live in brotherhood, enjoying equal rights and opportunities;

That only a democratic state, based on the will of all the people, can secure to all their birthright without distinction of colour, race, sex or belief;

And therefore, we the people of South Africa, black and white, together – equals, countrymen and brothers – adopt this Freedom Charter. And we pledge ourselves to strive together, sparing nothing of our strength and courage, until the democratic changes here set out have been won.

THE PEOPLE SHALL GOVERN!

Every man and woman shall have the right to vote for and stand as a candidate for all bodies which make laws;

All the people shall be entitled to take part in the administration of the country;

The rights of the people shall be the same regardless of race, colour, or sex;

All bodies of minority rule, advisory boards, councils and authorities shall be replaced by democratic organs of self-government.

ALL NATIONAL GROUPS SHALL HAVE EQUAL RIGHTS!

There shall be equal status in the bodies of state, in the courts, and in the schools, for all national groups and races;

All people shall have equal rights to use their own language and to develop their own folk culture and customs;

All national groups shall be protected by law against insults to their race and national pride;

The preaching and practice of national, race or colour discrimination and contempt shall be a punishable crime;

All apartheid laws and practices shall be set aside.

THE PEOPLE SHALL SHARE IN THE
COUNTRY'S WEALTH!

The national wealth of our country, the heritage of all South Africans, shall be restored to the people;

The mineral wealth beneath the soil, the banks and monopoly industry shall be transferred to the ownership of the people as a whole;

All other industries and trade shall be controlled to assist the well-being of the people;

All people shall have equal rights to trade where they choose, to manufacture and to enter all trades, crafts and professions.

THE LAND SHALL BE SHARED AMONG THOSE WHO
WORK IT!

Restrictions of land ownership on a racial basis shall be ended, and all the land re-divided amongst those who work for it, to banish famine and land hunger;

The state shall help the peasants with implements, seed, tractors and dams to save the soil and assist the tillers;

Freedom of movement shall be guaranteed to all who work on the land;

All shall have the right to occupy land wherever they choose;

People shall not be robbed of their cattle, and forced labour and farm prisons shall be abolished.

ALL SHALL BE EQUAL BEFORE THE LAW!

No one shall be imprisoned, deported or restricted without a fair trial;

No one shall be condemned by the order of any government official;

The courts shall be representatives of all the people;

Imprisonment shall be only for serious crime against the people, and shall aim at re-education; not vengeance;

All laws which discriminate on grounds of race, colour or belief shall be repealed.

ALL SHALL ENJOY EQUAL HUMAN RIGHTS!

The law shall guarantee to all their right to speak, to organize, to meet together, to publish, to preach, to worship and to educate their children;

The privacy of the house from police raids shall be protected by the law;

All shall be free to travel without restriction from countryside to town, from province to province, and from South Africa abroad;

Pass laws, permits and all other laws restricting these freedoms shall be abolished.

THERE SHALL BE WORK AND SECURITY!

All who work shall be free to form trade unions, to elect their officers and to make wage agreements with their employers;

The state shall recognize the right and duty of all to work and to draw full unemployment benefits;

Men and women of all races shall receive equal pay for equal work;

There shall be a forty-hour working week, a national minimum wage, paid annual leave, and sick leave for all workers, and maternity leave on full pay for all working mothers;

Miners, domestic workers, farm workers and civil servants shall have the same rights as all others who work;

Child labour, compound labour, the tot system and contract labour shall be abolished.

THE DOORS OF LEARNING AND OF CULTURE SHALL BE OPENED!

The government shall discover, develop and encourage national talent for the enhancement of our cultural life;

All the cultural treasures of mankind shall be open to all, by free exchange of books, ideas and contact with other lands;

The aim of education shall be to teach the youth to love their people and their culture, to honour human brotherhood, liberty and peace;

Education shall be free, compulsory, universal and equal for all children;

Higher education and technical training shall be opened to all by means of state allowances and scholarships awarded on the basis of merit;

Adult illiteracy shall be ended by a mass state education plan;

Teachers shall have all the rights of other citizens;

The colour bar in cultural life, in sport and in education shall be abolished.

THERE SHALL BE HOUSES, SECURITY AND COMFORT!

All people shall have the right to live where they choose, to be decently housed, and to bring up their families in comfort and security;

Unused housing space to be made available to the people;

Rent and prices shall be lowered, food plentiful and no one shall go hungry;

A preventive health scheme shall be run by the state;

Free medical care and hospitalization shall be provided for all, with special care for mothers and young children;

Slums shall be demolished, and new suburbs built where all have transport, roads, lighting, playing fields, crèches and social centres;

The aged, the orphans, the disabled and the sick shall be cared for by the state;

Rest, leisure and recreation shall be the right of all;

Fenced locations and ghettos shall be abolished, and laws which break up families shall be repealed.

THERE SHALL BE PEACE AND FRIENDSHIP!

South Africa shall be a full independent state which respects the rights and sovereignty of all nations;

South Africa shall strive to maintain world peace and the settlement of all international disputes by negotiation – not war;

Peace and friendship amongst all our people shall be secured by upholding the equal rights, opportunities and status of all;

The people of the protectorates – Basutoland, Bechuanaland and Swaziland – shall be free to decide for themselves their own future;

The right of all the people of Africa to independence and self-government shall be recognized, and shall be the basis of close co-operation.

Let all who love their people and their country now say, as we say here:

'THESE FREEDOMS WE WILL FIGHT FOR, SIDE BY SIDE, THROUGHOUT OUR LIVES, UNTIL WE HAVE WON OUR LIBERTY.'

WINNIE MANDELA'S BANNING ORDER

TO: NOMZAMO WINNIE MANDELA
(IN 3981073)
8115 ORLANDO
JOHANNESBURG

Notice in terms of Section 9(1) of the Internal Security Act, 1950 (Act 44 of 1950)

Whereas I, James Thomas Kruger, Minister of Justice, am satisfied that you engage in activities which endanger or are calculated to endanger the maintenance of public order, I hereby, in terms of section 9(1) of the Internal Security Act, 1950, prohibit you for a period commencing on the date on which this notice is delivered or tendered to you and expiring on 31 December 1981, from attending within the Republic of South Africa or the territory of South-West Africa –

(1)   any gathering contemplated in paragraph (a) of the said section 9(1); or
any gathering contemplated in paragraph (b) of the said section 9(1), of the nature, class or kind set out below:
(a)   Any social gathering, that is to say, any gathering at which the persons present also have social intercourse with one another;

(2)   being within –
(a)   any Bantu area, that is to say –
(i)   any Scheduled Bantu Area as defined in the Bantu Land Act, 1913 (Act 27 of 1913);
(ii)   any land of which the South African Bantu Trust referred to in section 4 of the Bantu Trust and Land Act, 1936 (Act 18 of 1936), is the registered owner or any land held in trust for a Bantu Tribal Community in terms of the said Bantu Trust and Land Act 1936;
(iii)   any location, Bantu hostel or Bantu village defined and set apart under the Bantu (Urban Areas) Consolidation Act, 1945 (Act 25 of 1945);
(iv)   any area approved for the residence of Bantu in terms of section 9(2)(h) of the Bantu (Urban Areas) Consolidation Act,

1945 (Act 25 of 1945);

(v) any Bantu Township established under the Regulations for the Administration and Control of Townships in Bantu Areas, promulgated in Proclamation R293 of 16 November 1962.

except Orlando;

(b) any Bantu compound;

(c) any area set apart under any law for the occupation of Coloured or Asiatic persons;

(d) the premises of any factory as defined in the Factories, Machinery and Building Work Act, 1941 (Act 22 of 1941);

(e) any place which constitutes the premises on which any publication as defined in the Internal Security Act, 1950, is prepared, compiled, printed or published;

(f) any place which constitutes the premises of any organization contemplated in Government Notice R2130 of 28 December 1962, as amended by Government Notice R1947 of 27 November 1964, and any place which constitutes premises on which the premises of any such organization are situate;

(g) any place or area which constitutes the premises on which any public or private university, university college, college, school or other educational institution is situate;

(h) any place or area which constitutes the premises of any superior or inferior court as defined in the Criminal Procedures Act, 1955 (Act 56 of 1955), except for the purpose of –

(i) applying to a magistrate for an exception to any prohibition in force against you under the Internal Security Act, 1950;

(ii) attending any criminal proceedings in which you are required to appear as an accused or a witness;

(iii) attending any civil proceedings in which you are a plaintiff, petitioner, applicant, defendant, respondent or other party or in which you are required to appear as a witness;

(3) performing any of the following acts –

(a) preparing, compiling, printing, publishing, disseminating or transmitting in any manner whatsoever any publications as defined in the Internal Security Act, 1950;

(b) participating or assisting in any manner whatsoever in the preparation, compilation, printing, publication, dissemination or transmission of any publication as so defined;

(c) contributing, preparing, compiling or transmitting in any manner whatsoever any matter for publication in any publication as so defined;

(d)   assisting in any manner whatsoever in the preparation, compilation or transmission of any matter for publication in any publication as so defined;

(e)   (i)   preparing, compiling, printing, publishing, disseminating or transmitting in any manner whatsoever any document (which shall include any book, pamphlet, record, list, placard, poster, drawing, photograph or picture which is not a publication within the meaning of paragraph 3(a) above); or

(ii)   participating or assisting in any manner whatsoever in the preparation, compilation, printing, publication, dissemination or transmission of any such document, in which, *inter alia* –

(aa)   any form of state or any principle or policy of the government of a state is propagated, defended, attacked, criticized, discussed or referred to;

(bb)   any matter is contained concerning any body, organization, group or association of persons, institution, society or movement which has been declared an unlawful organization by or under the Internal Security Act, 1950, or the Unlawful Organizations Act, 1960 (Act 34 of 1960), or any organization contemplated in Government Notice R2130 of 28 December 1962, as amended by Government Notice R1947 of 27 November 1964; or

(cc)   any matter is contained which is likely to engender feelings of hostility between the White and the non-White inhabitants of the Republic of South Africa;

(f)   giving any educational instruction in any manner or form to any person other than a person of whom you are a parent;

(g)   taking part in any manner whatsoever in the activities or affairs of any organization contemplated in Government Notice R2130 of 28 December 1962, as amended by Government Notice R1947 of 27 November 1964;

(4)   communicating in any manner whatsoever with any person whose name appears on any list in the custody of the officer referred to in section 8 of the Internal Security Act, 1950, or in respect of whom any prohibition under the Internal Security Act, 1950, or the Riotous Assemblies Act, 1956 (Act 17 of 1956), is in force;

(5)   receiving at the said residential premises any visitor other than –
(a)   a medical practitioner for medical attendance on you or members of your household, if the name of such medical practitioner does not appear on any list in the custody of the officer referred to in section 8 of the Internal Security Act, 1950, and no prohibition under the Internal Security Act, 1950, or the Riotous Assemblies Act, 1956, is in force in respect of such medical practitioner;
(b)   your children Zenani and Zindziswa.

Given under my hand at *Cape Town* this *23rd* day of *December, 1976*.

MINISTER OF JUSTICE

NOTE: The Magistrate, Johannesburg, has in terms of section 10(1)(a) of Act 44 of 1950 been empowered to authorize exceptions to the prohibitions contained in this notice.

Appendix

CONDITIONS OF VISIT TO NELSON MANDELA ON ROBBEN ISLAND

—Mr/Mrs/—Miss *W.... Man-dela*

.........*Voortrekker Street*..........

...............*Brandfort*...............

....................*9400*....................

The Commanding Officer

Prison Command

Private Bag ROBBEN ISLAND

7400

..............................*1–2–*19*79*.....

—Sir/Madam

APPLICATION FOR A PERMIT TO VISIT PRISONER

NO................................*466/64: N. Mandela*................................

Leave to visit Robben Island on the ....*10–2–*19*79*..... for the purpose as requested is granted to the following persons:

(a) ....*W. MANDELA*.........   I.D.No. ....*396873*...........

(b) ....   I.D.No. ....

A permit authorizing the visit has been forwarded to the Embarkation Officer, Cape Town Docks.

Children under the age of 16 years will, however, not be permitted to visit their relatives/friends on Robben Island.

You are requested to have your Identification Card with you to identify yourself to the Embarkation Officer.

You are further informed that only in offering irrefutable proof of identity will the visit be allowed to commence, failing to comply will result in the cancellation of the visit forthwith.

The boat leaves from Quay No. 5 at .*13.h.00*. and arrives back at Cape Town at .*17.h.45*.

Yours faithfully

for COMMANDING OFFICER

NOTE: This permit is valid only subject to you obtaining permission from the Magistrate at Brandfort to leave your residential area to travel to Robben Island for the sole purpose of visiting your husband.

CONDITIONS WITH WHICH WINNIE MANDELA
HAD TO COMPLY TO TRAVEL FROM
BRANDFORT TO ROBBEN ISLAND AND BACK

DEPARTEMENT VAN JUSTISIE –
DEPARTMENT OF JUSTICE

REPUBLIEK VAN SUID-AFRIKA – REPUBLIC OF SOUTH
AFRICA

Telegramadres: 'LANDDROS'
Telegraphic Address:
'MAGISTRATE'
Telefoonommer
Telephone No. ....¹.................

Reference No.

.........................11/5/2/1.........................
Verwysingsnommer

Privaatsak
Private Bag No. ....X10...............

Postkode
Postal Code ....9400............................

Mrs N. W. Mandela
802 Black Township
BRANDFORT
9400

LANDDROSKANTOOR
MAGISTRATE'S OFFICE
BRANDFORT
3rd June 1980

Madam

With reference to your application dated 26/5/80 you are hereby granted permission to leave the municipal area of Brandfort on Friday 6/6/80 for the sole purpose of proceeding to Cape Town in order to visit your husband on Robben Island on 7 and 8/6/80 provided that:

a)   You do not leave your place of residence at 802 Brandfort Black Township before 17 h 00 on 6/6/80
b)   You report to the Police at Brandfort Police Station before departure from and on return to Brandfort
c)   You make use of flight SA 329 which is scheduled to leave JBM Hertzog Airport, Bloemfontein for Cape Town at 19 h 10 and that you restrict your movements to the said JBM Hertzog Airport
d)   You return from Cape Town on 8/6/80 to Bloemfontein by flight 326 which is scheduled to leave Cape Town at 18 h 20

on 8/6/8o

e)   You take the shortest routes between your place of residence and the said J B M Hertzog Airport and back

f)   You report to the Police at Caledon Square on arrival at and before departure from Cape Town and restrict your movements to the said D F Malan Airport, Caledon Square Police Station, the harbour area and the place of residence of Dr Ayesha Ahmed at 39th Avenue, Elsiesrivier, and also that you take the shortest routes between these places

g)   You arrange with the Prison officials at Robben Island for the visit on 7 and 8/6/8o

h)   You return directly to your house at Brandfort Black Township as soon as possible after the arrival of your plane at J B M Hertzog Airport and that you again restrict your movements to the airport and

i)   You abide strictly by the remaining conditions of your restriction notices.

Yours faithfully

MAGISTRATE/BRANDFORT
(Mrs E J M Niemann)